The
Eating Well
Cookbook

The Eating Well
Cookbook

by John Doerper

Pacific Search Press

To Victoria,
with love and a raised glass
of northwest wine

Pacific Search Press, 222 Dexter Avenue North,
    Seattle, Washington 98109
© 1984 by John Doerper. All rights reserved
Printed in the United States of America

Edited by Marlene Blessing
Designed by Judy Petry

Cover: *Author shopping at Verdi's Farm Fresh Produce stand in Seattle's Pike Place Market*
(Don Anderson)

Library of Congress Cataloging in Publication Data

Doerper, John.
    The eating well cookbook.

    Includes index.
    1. Cookery, American—Northwest, Pacific.
1. Title.
TX715.D657 1984   641.59795   84-12101
ISBN 0-914718-93-2 (pbk.)

Contents

Acknowledgments

The recipes collected in this volume come largely from my own recipe files. Some are of obscure origin. Others were given me by friends. I have given credit wherever possible, but there are some recipes that have been in my files for so long that their sources are as remote as those of legends. To make sure I have not slighted anyone by including a recipe without proper credit (though I modify almost all recipes for my personal use), I would like to cite the following inspirations:

M. F. K. Fisher, Waverly Root, Evan Jones, James Beard, Craig Claiborne, Pierre Franey, Brillat-Savarin, André Simon, Elizabeth David, and Julia Child. And, of course, there are such classics as *The Joy of Cooking, The American Woman's Cookbook,* and *The New Larousse Gastronomique.*

As for the making of this book, I want to thank my editor at Pacific Search Press, Marlene Blessing, whose nose wrinkled at the mention of sea urchin roe, but who toughed it out through it all. Also, a thank you to the other worthy members of that staff, who have proven that small regional presses *can* help an author with an interesting manuscript make a splash.

Introduction

I always carry a corkscrew, an oyster knife, and a folding knife in the glove compartment of my car. They see a lot of use. The folding knife is no ordinary pocketknife; it is a precision tool with a highly tempered carbon steel blade (which can be honed to perfection on a beach pebble in a pinch) and a warm pearwood handle, shaped to fit the hand. It is a French Opinel, the kind of knife French three-star chef Paul Bocuse uses in his kitchen instead of the common, swordlike chef's knife.

My oyster knife has a stainless steel blade; lesser blades (and even carbon blades) tend to rust when subjected to salty oyster juices and to the rude handling of the road. While the folding knife has only one function, to cut, the oyster knife has many, from digging cockles out of gravelly beaches to opening cans of olive oil. It is mostly used for opening oysters, of course, for I cannot pass an oyster farm without buying at least a dozen of these succulent molluscs.

Oysters must be consumed in style. That's where the corkscrew comes in. Once I have a goodly supply of oysters, the next country market will supply me with wine, and I need only pull into a quiet spot—I already have fresh bread and lemons aboard—find a fallen log or mossy boulder for my picnic table and, in no time at all, a truly Lucullan feast is ready. Freshly baked bread (with perhaps a little country butter or cheese), plump oysters, and a dry wine—what more can a traveler want?

Any oysters I do not eat on the spot go into the ice chest. I always carry at least one ice chest in the trunk of my car, for I do much of my shopping while I am on the road: traveling for me is a moving feast. No matter how far I travel, whether only a few miles into the country or throughout Washington, British Columbia, and Oregon, there are always delectable foods to be found that are unobtainable at home—at least not with the same degree of freshness. Needless to say, oysters, clams, and mussels are much fresher bought on location than they can ever be at the hometown fishmonger's. Or I may trap some crawfish or catch a mess of local crabs (whether tiny beach crabs or large Dungeness), gather cockles, mussels, clams, sea cucumbers or urchins, or wet my line in rivers and lakes, hoping to catch some fish. On British Columbia's Sunshine Coast (or in the seafood markets of Vancouver), I look for freshly caught prawns or pink swimming scallops; in Seattle's Pike Place Market, I look for large red sea urchins and live geoduck and razor clams; on the Hood Canal, I buy fresh shrimp—caught that very day.

I do not have the willpower to pass a small-town bakery. I am swayed by the heady aroma of oven-fresh breads, pastries, and cookies, and I buy whatever smells and looks best to me (usually a country loaf of bread or a crisp baguette to go with my oysters). Then there are farmer's markets and roadside produce stands, selling seasonal fruits and vegetables picked that morning—delicate greens, glossy zucchini, crunchy carrots, crisp beans and peas, sun-warmed peaches and apricots, juicy cherries and plums, fragrant pears, and firm mountain apples. And apple cider, freshly squeezed apple cider (the kind you thought your great-great-grandparents used to make out on the farm, wherever that may have been). And I never forget the honeys, smooth filtered honeys or rough country honeys, made by local bees from coast, mountain, or desert wild flowers.

I also buy dairy products on the road: milk, cream, butter, buttermilk, and cheese. This is how I discovered the multitudinous varieties of buttermilk available in the Northwest (as though each small-town dairy had to have its own taste!) and the large selection of regional cheeses. Some of these cheeses, like the Camembert made by Blue Heron in Tillamook or the extrasharp Cheddars made in Tillamook, Bandon, and the Rogue River Valley, you cannot find anywhere else. Others, like the Okanogan Highlands goat cheese from Sally Jackson's tiny mountain farm, the excellent Sicamous Cheddar from British Columbia's Shuswap country, Pleasant Valley Gouda from Ferndale, Washington, and the Briar Hills goat cheeses from Chehalis are hard to find even a few miles from the cheese plants.

During these food forays, I continue to be amazed by the great variety and the excellence of the foods available to Northwesterners. And it seems that every time I take a trip, I discover something new: a specially treated country ham, perhaps, or smoked sausages, or a new style of meltingly tender smoked oysters, a new variety of apple, a new grower of succulent vegetables, a new cheese maker, a newly opened winery. So many exciting things continually happen, it's a challenge to keep up with the latest developments.

During the last several years, Americans across the continent, plus an ever-increasing number of visitors from Asia and Europe, have visited the Northwest to enjoy the unparalleled scenic beauty of our region. These same visitors have thoroughly enjoyed the superb foods, wines, and beers the Northwest produces, spreading their fame to other areas. In an early 1984 visit to the area, French wine expert Armand Cottin commented on the quality of our foods, past and present, by saying that we've always had the greatest of raw materials available to us in the Pacific Northwest—and that we were finally learning how to use them "properly." M. Cottin, like other visitors, feels that the quality of both home and restaurant cooking in the Pacific Northwest has blossomed dramatically in the last decade or so.

The Eating Well Cookbook is meant to be a salute to that blossoming, an ode to a region whose time has surely come.

The Basics

Northwest Fresh

No matter how quick and easy modern methods of transportation have become, the best and tastiest foods are found at their source. Foods, no matter how well they are handled, seem to suffer from a kind of "transportation shock" when they are sent away from home (this does not, of course, apply to such sturdy comestibles as cheese).

I have been fortunate in being able to look to the many excellent markets (whether commercial, public, or farmers') of the Pacific Northwest for the ingredients I use in my cookery, and I have bought much of my produce, fish, shellfish, and meat directly at the source—from a fisherman, vegetable or fruit grower, dairyman, or rancher. There are always new products coming into the market, whether new cheese or different oysters. Try them all—your neighborhood may harbor a small producer whose products are of world-class quality, despite their limited distribution.

In the Pacific Northwest, we have ready access to superb fresh vegetables and fruits, fish, crabs, shrimp, and crawfish, to excellent oysters, clams, wild berries, and world-class wines. Nowhere else in the country are all of these exquisite foods found in such proximity to each other; nowhere else can you dig clams or trap crabs in the morning, buy cheese from a cottage-industry cheese maker at noon, and pick wild alpine blueberries in the afternoon. And in only a few regions of the country can you accompany such sumptuous food with locally made wines and beers. Things are truly looking up for the connoisseur of good foods and drink in the Northwest.

With the help of friends, I often have foraged, fished, or hunted for many of the wild foods of the Pacific Northwest. In this book, however, I have tried to restrict the more esoteric ingredients called for in some of my recipes to foods readily available in season at either the Granville Island Market in Vancouver, at Seattle's Pike Place Market, at our seasonal farmers' markets, or at oriental seafood markets.

People often ask me how I learned to eat such "weird" seafoods as sea urchins, barnacles, and sea cucumbers. Mostly I was introduced to these tasty foods by friends. Sometimes I stumbled over them by accident. I have found, at least for myself, that the idea of eating a particular food can affect the mind much more violently than eating the actual food will affect the stomach. This was certainly true the first time I tried Chinese sea cucumber. I was enjoying a dinner with friends at a restaurant in Vancouver's Chinatown, and one of the dishes we ordered included both sea cucumber pieces and chunks of black mushroom. I carefully pushed the mushrooms aside (I was sure these were the sea cucumbers) and ate the black sea cucumber pieces with relish. Commenting to my friends on the good taste of these "mushrooms," they wryly asked me how I could tell since I hadn't eaten any of them yet.

Needless to say, once my stomach had accepted sea cucumbers as a tasty food, my mind followed suit. I have enjoyed sea cucumbers ever since. But you should never eat anything unless you like its taste—no matter how much hype has gone into promoting it. Yet you should try to remain open to experimenting with new foods. How else will you know what tasty treats you have passed up?

In most of the recipes given in this book, you can make substitutions and introduce experiments of your own. No recipe is rigidly laid down or meant to be followed slavishly. Use the recipes as a starting point or springboard, then introduce variations of your own. The flavor may be different from the original recipe's, but it may be just as good or even better. Most of all, remember that cooking is fun and the Northwest's unique bounty can enhance any kitchen experiment you may have in mind!

Odd Ingredients

While I'm willing to concede that the ingredients I list here are deemed "odd" by many people, they are a commonplace part of my daily fare. Over the years I've lived in the Pacific Northwest, I have rooted relentlessly to find out what foodstuffs are available and where they can be found. Detailed information about sources for these ingredients is given in the Appendix of my first book, *Eating Well: A Guide to Foods of the Pacific Northwest* (Pacific Search Press).

If you aren't feeling quite as adventurous, or simply haven't the time and energy to gather ingredients like the ones I recommend in my recipes, please consult this listing to see what recommendations I make for substitutions. And, of course, you can always use your imagination and improvise solutions for ingredients you don't have at hand. Remember, recipes are not meant to be inviolate.

Fruits, Vegetables, and Fungi

One brief warning. Be sure that you consult an experienced mushroomer if you decide to forage for some of the mushrooms I mention here. Some of the most innocent-looking mushrooms can be toxic and cause more than just your recipe to fail!

Alaria. Alaria is a tasty seaweed with a long, olive green to rich brown terminal blade rising from a short stipe. It is quite common in the lower intertidal zone on moderate to very exposed rocky shores. Collect your own, buy it dried in oriental markets, or use dried *Nori* as a substitute.

Azuki (or Adzuki). A sweetish red oriental bean that makes excellent sprouts.

Borage Flowers. Both the large leaves and the small blue flowers of this tall annual plant are edible. The leaves have somewhat of a cucumberish taste and can be used to garnish a number of foods, from appetizers to main courses to the cheese course (all but sweet desserts). Borage is widely grown in gardens (and may be bought at farmers' markets) and it grows occasionally in the wild throughout the lowlands west of the Cascades. Use other edible flowers as a substitute if borage flowers are unavailable.

Bracken. The fiddleheads of this fern can be cooked like asparagus after they have been cleaned of their brownish fuzz. Bracken grows in semidry woodlands, pastures, and fields. It may be collected in spring in the lowlands, later in the mountains.

Brambleberry. The young thick shoots of blackberries, thimbleberries, salmonberries, etc. They may be peeled and cooked like asparagus. Available in early spring in the lowlands, then increasingly later in the highlands as the snow melts in the mountains and growth sets in.

Burdock. This sticky-seeded weed grows in weed lots throughout the Northwest. The Japanese dig up the root and use it in a number of dishes. You can dig your own burdock or buy it in oriental food stores as *gobo*. (Digging up the long, slender root can be a frustrating task.)

Cattail Hearts. These are the very pale (sometimes almost white) centers of fresh cattail shoots, collected when the cattails are very young (about a foot or two in height). The light-colored, slightly mucilaginous core and the pale green leaves surrounding it may be cooked like asparagus (boiled for five minutes; steamed for fifteen) or sliced and served raw in salads. Cut the shoots very close to the rootstocks when collecting cattails (or close to the soil if the rootstock is buried). Discard all coarse outer leaves; leaves too tough to eat raw don't seem to tenderize much in cooking. You may use canned bamboo shoots as a substitute, but the taste will not be as fine.

Chickweed. This tender little plant thrives in disturbed soils, waste lots, and gardens. It adds a nice touch to salads (avoid very hairy species). Chickweed survives frosts that kill other annuals. It is thus a perfect midwinter salad green.

Chinese Vegetables. Such exotic vegetables as bok choy (also called bok toy), choy sum, gai choy (Chinese mustard), gai lan (Chinese "broccoli"), and lo-bak have become quite common in our markets. All should be used when very small. The huge bok choy for sale in our supermarkets are too large and coarse to be really good. Try the tiny bundles of bok choy sold in Chinese markets and at some farmers' markets instead—you'll taste the difference. All of these Chinese vegetables may be used interchangeably, and they all benefit from a light soy sauce or oyster sauce dressing. Fresh, northwest-grown Chinese vegetables are generally available from May through September.

Chrysanthemums. Another oriental vegetable that's becoming more popular in the Northwest, edible chrysanthemums are much milder in taste than their flower garden relatives. Lawn daisies, oxeye daisies, and Shasta daisies are also edible, and their flowers may be used as garnishes (but the taste can be very strong at times). Edible chrysanthemums are available from summer through fall and sometimes into winter.

Collards. This is a relative of kale, with a less refined taste. Try farmers' markets for the best.

Daikon. This large Japanese radish (smaller, thinner versions are called icicle radishes) has become very popular. It can be found almost everywhere, from supermarkets to sushi parlors. Daikon is a bit hotter than ordinary radishes, but also has a nicer flavor. It can be eaten raw, cooked, and used for garnishes.

Dandelions. Dandelions should be picked early in spring, before the plant has flowered. They become too bitter in taste as they get older. The bitterness may be boiled out, but it's hardly worth it. The fresh young greens are a pleasant addition to salads, however.

Endive. Both curly and broad-leaved endive (escarole) do better in cool climates, though they can also tolerate heat better than other lettuces. Northwest endives should be in the markets from mid-May through September.

Enokitake Mushrooms. A skinny, light-colored Japanese mushroom that grows in clusters and looks somewhat like fat matchsticks. They have a delicate flavor and may be eaten raw or sautéed like champignon.

Filberts. *See Hazelnuts*

Hazelnuts. The Northwest grows just about the entire U.S. crop of this nut. I like to use these in many recipes instead of the commonly called for almonds, pistachios, or peanuts. A good northwest hazelnut is bound to improve many a dish, from appetizers to desserts.

Hops. A tasty vegetable that tastes like asparagus but is, unfortunately, not as widely available as it should be. Substitute asparagus.

Horse Mushrooms. A large, fleshy, and very flavorful agaricus (with a flavor of anise), found in fields and meadows in spring and fall.

Kale. A curly-leaved, late season cabbage. It tastes best after the first frost. Some of the best kale I've ever tasted I first had to dig out from underneath a foot of snow.

Kohlrabi. A peculiar cabbage with a swollen stem. Best when the "bulbs" are about two to three inches in diameter; they toughen if they grow much larger. This cool-climate vegetable may be sliced like a cucumber or cooked like turnips.

Lamb's-lettuce. A European salad plant widely grown throughout the Pacific Northwest in home and truck gardens. Lamb's-lettuce, also known as mâche or corn salad, has small, sweet leaves up to about an inch long. If you cannot find lamb's-lettuce, use romaine lettuce as a substitute.

Lamb's-quarters. A widely distributed "weed" of excellent taste. It may be used in salads, soups, or as a steamed vegetable. The younger the leaves, the better. Related to spinach but higher in protein. Available from spring to fall.

Lotus Root. A bland-tasting aquatic tuber with a picturesque core. It is increasingly found in northwest markets. Good for garnishes.

Matsutake. A pine mushroom that is most common in the Northwest, where it is free for the picking. It brings an amazingly high price in Japan, where it is highly treasured. Some gourmets like it for its taste, some like it because it is expensive, some don't like it at all. You'll have to find your own unless you're willing to spend a lot more money than it is worth. Substitute shiitake or dried Chinese mushrooms.

Meadow Mushrooms. Lovely, tasty, delicate, easily gathered relatives of our common commercial champignon, with a much better flavor. Use commercial button mushrooms if you can't find the wild cousin.

Nasturtiums. Leaves, buds, and flowers of this pretty garden plant are edible (make sure they have not been sprayed with a pesticide). The leaves may be used raw in salads or cooked as a sorrel substitute in soups; the buds may be pickled like capers; the multicolored flowers make beautiful edible garnishes.

Nettles. Young nettles, picked before the stringy flowers appear and the plant toughens, are an excellent spring potherb. Make sure to wear gloves when collecting them. Use them instead of spinach.

Nori. Also called laver, this seaweed is sold in square sheets (and is available in just about all of our supermarkets). It may be used for making sushi and as a substitute for fresh seaweed.

Orache. Also called garden orache. This plant is grown in a few northwest gardens. Look for it in farmers' markets. If you cannot find any, substitute saltbush (found in salt marshes and inland alkali flats). Orache is cooked with sorrel to balance the sorrel's acidity and to maintain the green color of sorrel in cooking. It is not absolutely necessary in a recipe—it may be left out, as long as an equal amount of sorrel is substituted.

Oyster Mushrooms. A tangy mushroom which is now grown commercially in southern British Columbia and northwestern Washington. May be used in lieu of shiitake mushrooms.

The Prince. A noble agaricus of excellent flavor. This meaty mushroom is found in lawns, flower beds, orchards, and along roadsides from June to October. Use it in lieu of the less tasty commercial mushroom.

Quince. A bland fruit when fresh, it becomes sublime in jams, jellies, and compotes (and turns pink as well). Found at farmers' markets, public markets, and roadside stands each fall throughout our region.

Radicchio. A red-leaved Italian chicory. If it's not in your garden and if you cannot find it in your market, use endive, chicory, or escarole instead.

Red Huckleberry. Tart relatives of our sweet blueberries and sour cranberries. The airy shrubs are found in lowland woods (and even city parks) throughout the Pacific Northwest. You'll have to gather your own, a very easy task. Wild cranberries make an acceptable substitute.

Rocket (Arugula). This tangy potherb adds zest to salads and vegetable dishes. You should be able to find it in your favorite farmers' or public market. Or use spinach, dandelion, or any of the wild cabbage greens instead.

Rutabagas. This is by some considered to be a more obnoxious cousin of the turnip; others think of it as a delicious root vegetable. Rutabagas store well in the ground and taste better after they have undergone a few chilling experiences. Prepare them like turnips. They're available from mid-June all the way to February or even March.

Salmonberry Shoots. These tender green vines as well as other berry shoots can be peeled when very young and cooked like asparagus.

Salsify. A root that is supposed to taste like oysters, but doesn't, yet still makes excellent soup. It can be left in the ground all winter, until spring, and harvested as needed.

Shiitake Mushrooms. A Japanese mushroom that is commonly available in dried form and increasingly as a fresh mushroom. Use the fresh whenever possible. Shiitake may be used in recipes calling for wild fungi.

Sprouts. A few years ago, we had nothing but mung bean sprouts available to us. Then came soybean sprouts and alfalfa sprouts. My favorite for eating raw is a mixture of mung, pea, azuki, and lentil sprouts. Fresh sprouts are available in just about every supermarket these days, but you'll find the best and freshest in oriental food stores.

Violets. Both leaves and flowers are edible. Use the tender green leaves in spring salads and the sweet flowers for garnishes. They go well with just about anything from appetizers to desserts.

Wild Cranberries. These tastier and smaller relatives of the commercial cranberry may be used in all dishes calling for cranberry. But you'll have to pick your own in coastal bogs.

Zillah Chilies. Just about any chili pepper you can think of (and quite a few you've probably never heard of) are grown in the Yakima Valley. These chilies are milder (because the weather isn't as hot) than the chilies grown in the Southwest, but they are much more flavorful (our long summer days extend the growing season).

Fresh mild chilies should be peeled before they are used in cooking. This is best done by roasting or charring (some cookbooks call for submerging them in hot oil, but this spoils their texture and makes them greasy). I have found that charring them over a hot burner (I place a small grill about one inch above the heat) works best. The blacker and more blistered the skins, the easier they'll come off.

Poblanos (known as anchos when they are dried), bell peppers, jalapeños, serranos, and the small hot oriental peppers are among the best chilies we grow. Yellow wax peppers may range from very mild to quite torrid.

When handling fresh hot chilies, always make sure you don't squirt any of their juice into your eyes, and always wash your hands carefully after handling the hot ones—the incandescent juice tends to stick around.

Fish and Meat

Abalone. A delectable mollusc commonly available in specialty seafood stores as well as on some of our intertidal rocks. Overharvesting has made it somewhat scarce, however. The large flat foot is the part most commonly eaten. It may be pounded, to break down the fibers, and fried like a steak. Or it may be cut into thin strips and stir-fried. Or really fresh abalone may be presented in my favorite way, sliced and eaten raw as sashimi. The firm, liverlike roe may also be eaten.

Cabezon. A tasty fish of somewhat grotesque appearance. Caught regularly by sports fishermen, occasionally by commercial fishermen, and is sometimes available in seafood markets. Substitute rockfish if you cannot find cabezon; it's almost as tasty (and it is commonly sold as red snapper or rock cod in your supermarket or fish shop).

Carp. A freshwater fish that can have a luscious taste when caught in clean (nonmuddy) waters and when it is prepared as soon after it is caught as possible. It is very easy to catch (one reason for its popularity), but Chinese seafood markets carry a steady supply of very fresh carp.

Chinese Sausage. A specialty sausage sold in Chinese food markets and in some supermarkets (the best comes from Canada). There's really no equivalent, but you may use a fresh pepperoni if you can't find the real thing. Chinese sausage sautéed and cut into slices makes an excellent appetizer.

Cockles. Cockles are clamlike molluscs with multiridged shells living right below the surface of the tideflats. They are easily scooped up, or you can buy them in oriental seafood markets. Cockles may be cooked in chowders; the foot of the cockle is delicious served raw on sushi.

Fish Roe. Most fresh- and saltwater fish have edible roe (avoid sculpin roe; it is said to be toxic, though the fish themselves are not). Large-egged roe may be salted to make caviar; small-egged row may be gently poached or sautéed, scrambled with eggs, or smoked. Carp roe is a traditional ingredient in Greek *taramosalata.* Soft roe are the milt (sperm) of the male fish. They may be poached and are excellent in salads as a dressing.

Frog Legs. These tasty little morsels are the only part of the frog that is commonly eaten. You may catch your own (bullfrogs and green frogs are best), buy them fresh in Chinese fish markets, or buy them from a supermarket (though the latter may have only legs of uncertain age and ancestry). Both French-Canadians and Chinese are enthusiastic consumers of frog legs.

Geoducks. The biggest of northwest clams, in both size and taste. Immerse live clams in boiling water for a second, until skin loosens. Skin, shell, and gut. The siphon is a bit tough. It may be slit open, pounded, and fried as a steak or ground or chopped for chowder (my preferred method). The more tender belly meat may be served raw as sashimi or sushi or cooked and stir-fried. It is also excellent in salads, either raw or cooked.

Giant Acorn Barnacles. A northwest specialty much cherished by gourmet divers. Not commonly available in markets. Substitute regular barnacle meat, gooseneck barnacle stalks, or pink shrimp.

Leafy Hornmouth Snails. Mild-flavored intertidal molluscs found plentifully all along our coasts. If you're not into collecting your own, substitute the marine snails sold in Chinese seafood markets or cubed geoduck belly meat.

Limpets. Tasty, cone-shaped marine snails which graze on the thin film of algae covering tidal rocks. Collect your own or substitute abalone or geoduck belly meat.

Marine Snails. If you're averse to picking these tasty morsels off tidal rocks (or if you haven't got the time), buy them in Chinese seafood markets or substitute abalone, geoduck belly meat, or small clams.

Pea Crabs. Tiny, tasty, soft-shelled crabs that may be eaten whole. Most commonly found in large clams, horse mussels, and oysters. If clams are steamed open, the crabs need no further cooking. Or pea crabs may be sautéed in butter.

Pink (Swimming) Scallops. Small, very tasty free-swimming scallops found throughout the inland waters of Puget Sound, Washington Sound, Georgia Strait, and Juan de Fuca Strait. They must be absolutely fresh, and they are eaten whole, raw or steamed.

Prosciutto. Italian ham; you may use a good country ham instead.

Red Turban Snails. Tasty intertidal snails which you'll have to gather yourself. Substitute the marine snails found in Chinese seafood markets, geoduck belly meat, or small clams.

Rock Crab. A sweeter, though somewhat smaller, cousin of the Dungeness. Use interchangeably with the Dungeness.

Rock Scallops. Very large, delicately tasty relatives of the free-swimming scallop found in fish markets. You'll have to gather your own, or you may use other scallops as a substitute. But you'll miss a lot: many connoisseurs consider this to be our finest-tasting shellfish. Wild scallops may at times contain excellent, brightly colored roe for which there is no substitute. (Use salmon or golden whitefish caviar instead, for effect, if not for taste.)

Sculpin. *See Cabezon*

Sea Cucumbers. These common echinoderms may be gathered fresh in rocky shoreline areas at minus tides. When a recipe calls for only the internal muscles, scallops may be substituted. If a whole sea cucumber is called for, purchase from a Chinese seafood market either dried or presoaked.

Sea Perch. Small, tasty saltwater fish that may be cooked whole. Catch your own or buy them in seafood markets.

Sea Urchin and Its Roe. This spiny marine creature has long been a favorite with both Mediterranean and Japanese gourmets. Corsicans and Italians break off the top of the shell, dip bread inside, soaking up all of the contents. The Japanese prefer the orange gonads and roe, serving it on sushi. There's really no taste substitute for sea urchin roe. If you cannot find sea urchins in the wild, buy them at oriental seafood markets or at Seattle's Pike Place Market. Sea urchin roe should be consumed as fresh as possible, or it will lose its fruity taste. But in a pinch, you can buy salted roe at markets such as Seattle's Uwajimaya.

Shredded Jellyfish (Dried). An oriental delicacy with little flavor but a nice crunchy texture. It is added to salads to provide texture. It must be soaked, drained, and soaked for at least twenty-four hours to rid it of excess salt before it is marinated.

Sucker Roe. A tasty roe that you'll have to get yourself, unless you can find it in Chinese fish markets. Substitute golden whitefish caviar, steelhead caviar, or rockfish or carp roe if you are unable to find sucker roe.

Herbs and Spices

Chervil. A delicate, parsleylike herb. Unfortunately, it is not available in most of our markets (it is occasionally sold in farmers' markets and public markets). Chervil grows well in warm garden spots and in pots set into a sunny window.

Chinese Chives. A flat-leaved chive with a garlicky taste. Seasonally available in oriental food shops. May be used instead of garlic.

Elephant Garlic. A large-headed and large-cloved relative of our common garlic with a pleasant pungency of its own. It may be used as a substitute for common garlic and vice versa.

Fennel (Finocchio). This tangy herbaceous "bulb" can be served as an appetizer, in salads, or with fish and meat. It is generally ready in fall.

Gingerroot. The recipes in this book call for the fresh gingerroot sold in our markets. Do *not* use powdered ginger. If you cannot find fresh gingerroot in your market, substitute fresh lemon juice and freshly grated lemon zest.

Green Peppercorns. Unripe peppercorns with a unique flavor, quite unlike either black or white peppercorns (the more mature stages of the same spice). They come either bottled in water or brine or freeze-dried. I prefer the freeze-dried peppercorns, since they can be easily crushed in a mortar and have no pickling juice side taste.

Lovage. A flavorful garden herb that grows very well in the Northwest and may be used in lieu of celery.

Purslane (Portulaca). A very succulent and very common garden "weed" that is excellent in salads and soups.

Tellicherry Peppercorns. The best, most full-flavored variety of black pepper. Available from spice shops.

Sauces and Condiments

Aceto Balsamico. A special, sweet Italian vinegar; widely available in specialty stores and supermarkets. There's really no substitute, but Chinese sweet vinegar will do.

Capers. Capers are the pickled flower buds of a Mediterranean shrub. They are widely available in our food markets and delis. The smaller and firmer the buds are, the better. You may use nasturtium buds pickled in vinegar instead of the more expensive capers.

Chinese Chili Sauce. A thick, pungent sauce available in oriental markets and in some supermarkets. Use with caution, since its fieriness may increase in cooking. Tabasco sauce can serve as a reasonable substitute.

Chinese Red Vinegar. A specialty rice vinegar available in oriental markets and in some supermarkets. It is quite pale in color, like a rosé wine, and has a delicate flavor. It may be used in cooking or as a dip for noodles and seafood. Substitute red wine vinegar diluted with rosé wine.

Chinese Sour Mustard Greens. Also known as Chinese pickles or preserved mustard greens. These are a form of Chinese sauerkraut widely available in markets throughout our area. If you can't find any, use regular sauerkraut from which all the juice has been squeezed.

Hon-mirin. This is unsalted mirin. It is a sweet Japanese cooking wine and is available in supermarkets.

Hot Bean Paste. A fermented soybean paste with quite a bit of chili added. Available in cans in markets throughout the Pacific Northwest.

Mustards. The goopy ballpark mustard so beloved by American hot dog and hamburger eaters is not fit to be used for refined cooking. For one thing, there's too much turmeric in it. And its flavor is too coarse. Düsseldorf mustard or any of the French mustards (Dijon, Meaux, Pommery, etc.) that have no extra flavoring added (like green peppercorns) may be used interchangeably, though there may be some difference in taste.

Nuoc Mam. An oriental fish sauce that is to Vietnamese cooking what soy sauce is to Chinese cooking and salt is to western cooking. I like using this mild-flavored condiment in lieu of salt (because of its flavor, you need to use less salt). Look for the words Ca Com on the label, which mean that only anchovies were used in making the sauce, and for the word nhi which signifies a sauce of the highest quality. Both Vietnamese and Thai fish sauces are excellent. Philippine and Chinese fish sauces are too coarse. The Squid brand is best.

Pear Cider. A dry cider more commonly found in British Columbia than in the United States. It is excellent for some dishes. Use dry apple cider if you are unable to find pear cider.

Rice Vinegar. A pleasantly mild Japanese vinegar. Buy only the unflavored version.

Soy Sauce. This condiment, made from fermented soybeans, wheat, yeast, and salt, comes in three basic models:

Light (or thin) soy sauce, which is your basic, clear, pure soy sauce, light in color and quite salty (use in lieu of salt).

Japanese soy sauce, which is less salty and sweeter because it is made with more wheat.

Chinese heavy (or black) soy sauce, which is thickened with molasses. Most soy sauces on the market today are made by an accelerated process which allows the sauce to be made in three to four days instead of the four to six months minimum it takes to make a natural soy sauce. In this process, natural ingredients are replaced by hydrolyzed vegetable proteins, hydrochloric acid, caramel, and corn syrup. These sauces are too highly concentrated, of inferior taste, too salty, and often bitter. Look for the words "naturally fermented" on the label to avoid inferior sauces. My favorite is a naturally fermented Japanese soy sauce called *Marudai.*

Wasabi. This spicy green condiment is generally called Japanese horseradish, but it is unrelated to our white horseradish. It is more fragrant and less sharp. Fresh wasabi is hard to find in the Northwest, but you may use either wasabi paste (it comes in tubes and must be refrigerated after opening) or powdered wasabi. This comes in small cans and is mixed with water to make wasabi paste. The bitingly fresh taste of wasabi goes very well with raw fish dishes. Wasabi is served with sashimi and is spread on sushi between the rice pillow and the topping. It is also mixed with soy sauce to make a tasty dipping sauce for both sashimi and sushi.

Miscellany

Cascadian. A tangy goat cheese made by Briar Hills Dairy in Chehalis, Washington.

Duck Eggs. These eggs are larger and more flavorful than chicken eggs. They are commonly sold at farmers' markets, public markets, and in oriental markets (where you get to choose between fresh and pickled duck eggs). Or check the farmers' ads in your local newspaper.

Escargots. Our native escargots are the *petit gris* raised commercially on the Long Beach peninsula in southwestern Washington and in Oregon. If you cannot find the escargots fresh, use canned snails.

Fontina Cheese. A semihard Italian cheese widely sold in cheese shops. Use Pleasant Valley Gouda as a substitute.

Quail Eggs. These tiny eggs, which taste like chicken eggs, can be found fresh in oriental markets like Seattle's Uwajimaya. Canned quail eggs are an inferior substitute.

Sesame Oil. This oil is too strong for cooking; use it as a flavoring agent. Make sure to buy 100 percent pure Chinese sesame oil.

Sesame Seeds. These seeds come in both white and black. White sesame seeds should be gently toasted before being used to enhance their flavor.

Tofu. A bean curd that was hard to find, even in health food stores, just a decade or so ago; it is now widely available in supermarkets. It comes in soft and hard versions and has a delicate taste that is complemented by delicate sauces, but that is enhanced by flavorful sauces as well.

Sour Cream

Whipping cream   1 pint
Yogurt   1 teaspoon

1. Stir yogurt into whipping cream.
2. Let sit for a couple of days in a warm (but not hot) place.

Note: The best sour cream is made by letting unpasteurized cream (from a certified dairy) sour naturally at room temperature for a few days.

Variations: You may produce a quick sour cream by stirring a teaspoon of lemon juice into a pint of pasteurized whipping cream and letting it stand in a warm place for an hour or so.

Or blend a tablespoon of soured raw milk into a pint of pasteurized sour cream and let stand overnight.

Or substitute crème fraîche (see Index) for sour cream.

Makes about 1 pint

Unsalted Butter

The smallest amount of cream you should use for this would be 1 pint. Simply pour the cream into a food processor fitted with either a plastic or metal blade. Process. Cream will thicken and get slightly hard and yellow in the first stage. During the second (and final) stage, your machine will suddenly spin faster because the butterfat will have separated, making the mixture yellower, with a watery white liquid running through it. Remove your processor's work bowl to sink and drain butter in cheesecloth or muslin. Be sure to squeeze butter to remove excess liquid stored within. Voilà, you will have sweet, spreadable butter for cooking or smoothing over bread or crackers.

Basic Cream Cheese

Whole milk or half milk/half cream   2 quarts
Buttermilk (preferably Darigold or Tillamook)   4 tablespoons
Rennet   ¼-ounce packet
Water   1 tablespoon

1. Heat milk to 100°, add buttermilk, stir thoroughly, and cover pot. Let sit for a minimum of 2 hours. (The longer you leave it to culture, the stronger the final cheese will be.)
2. Dissolve rennet (available from health food and gourmet shops throughout the Northwest) with water in a cup.
3. Reheat "started" milk to 100°, stir in dissolved rennet, cover pot, and let rest for another 2 to 3 hours. After that time, a soft curd will have "set," or separated from the whey.
4. Line a colander or cheese mold with washed cheesecloth, gently spoon curds into mold, and let whey drain off for 8 to 10 hours in a cool room.
5. Scrape down curds clinging to sides of cheesecloth and fold down cheesecloth. If you use a mold, you may press down curds with a heavy jar that fits inside (gradually fill with water to slowly increase weight). If you use a colander, tie cheesecloth into a bag after most of the whey has drained and suspend cheese above a container to drain off more whey and to let it compact under its own weight.
6. The higher the cream content of milk mixture, the richer cheese will be—and the softer and more difficult to handle curd will be.

Makes 6 to 8 ounces

Crème Fraîche

Crème fraîche is the kind of thing culinary snobs like to veil in a cloud of mystery. There's really nothing to it, yet it is very essential in a number of tasty dishes. Here is Virginia Fuller's recipe.

Whipping cream   1 cup
Buttermilk (preferably Darigold or Tillamook)   1 cup

1. Mix cream and buttermilk.
2. Let stand and culture at room temperature for at least 8 hours.
3. Stir and refrigerate until needed.

Note: The longer you let it culture, the thicker it will be. If you make more than you can or want to use, pour the rest into your food processor and beat it with the steel blade until it turns into butter.

Makes 2 cups

Small Curd Cottage Cheese

Here is a quick cottage cheese recipe that makes very good cheese despite its simplicity. This is a rennetless cheese that will have a softer texture and smaller curd than a rennet-curdled cheese, but it has a pleasant sourish taste and will keep in the refrigerator for about 1 week. It is delicious when eaten alone, excellent with fresh fruit, and it may be used in any recipe calling for cottage cheese.

Skim milk   1 gallon
Buttermilk   4 tablespoons

1. Warm milk to 72°. Stir in buttermilk. Cover pot to set for 16 to 24 hours at 72°. (This is quite easy to do if you have heated your milk in a heavy clay pot. I like to use a large Chinese sandy pot which retains heat exceptionally well.)
2. After curd has coagulated, cut it into ¼-inch cubes and let it set for 15 minutes.
3. Raise temperature of curd 1 degree a minute until it reaches 100°. Stir every several minutes to keep curds from matting.
4. After keeping curds at 100° for 10 minutes and stirring regularly, raise temperature to 112° over a 15-minute period (again at a rate of about 1 degree a minute).
5. Hold temperature at 112° for 30 minutes or until curds are firm. (The test for firmness is very "scientific"; squeeze a curd particle between thumb and forefinger. If the curd has a custard consistency inside, it is not ready and should be cooked longer.)
6. When curds are cooked sufficiently, let them settle to bottom of pot for 5 minutes.
7. Carefully pour off the whey, making sure not to lose any curds.
8. Line a colander with cheesecloth and pour curds into it. Let them drain for several minutes. If a less sour cottage cheese is desired, curds can be washed by dipping the bag of cheesecloth into a bowl of cool water: dip curds several times and allow to drain for several minutes.

Next, rinse curds in a bowl of ice water to cool, and return bag to colander to drain for 5 minutes.

9. To salt and cream curds, place them in a bowl and break up any pieces that are matted together. Add several tablespoons of heavy cream to produce a creamier texture. Add salt to taste and blend well.

Variations: You may make a goat's milk cottage cheese in a similar fashion: follow the same steps as above, but add a small amount of rennet to the culture after the temperature has been raised to 72°, and do not raise the temperature over 102° when cooking the curds.

You may also press the curd to get a hard farmer's cheese. But it is better to make a hard cheese from a hard cheese recipe that calls for rennet—especially if you plan on aging the cheese.

Makes about 1½ pounds

Mayonnaise

This is simple to make and far superior to commercial mayonnaise. Better yet, this is really a foolproof recipe.

Large egg   1 or
   Egg yolks   3
Dijon-style mustard   1 teaspoon
Wine vinegar or lemon juice   1 tablespoon
Salad oil   1 cup
Salt and freshly ground black pepper   to taste

1. In blender or food processor, process egg, mustard, and vinegar for 3 seconds to blend well.
2. With blender still running, add oil, a few drops at a time at first, then increasing to a slow, steady stream about 1/16 inch wide. As you add oil, mayonnaise will thicken.
3. Taste and season with a few more drops of vinegar and salt and pepper, if desired.

Note: The key to making successful mayonnaise is to add the oil as slowly and evenly as possible. Also, part of the success of this recipe rests on your choosing a consistency and richness most pleasing to you. The whole egg mayonnaise is neither as stiff nor as rich as that made with egg yolks alone.

Makes 1 cup

Chicken Stock

Chicken carcass   1
Giblets
Small onion   1, grated
Small carrot   1, thinly sliced
Celery stalk   1, thinly sliced on bias
Cold water   3 quarts
Bay leaf   1
Lemon thyme   ⅛ teaspoon
Salt and freshly ground white pepper   ⅛ teaspoon each

1. Chop carcass into large pieces; place in stockpot. Coarsely chop giblets; sprinkle over chicken pieces. Add onion, carrot, and celery. Cover with cold water. Let rest for 5 to 10 minutes.
2. Bring to a boil over high heat; skim froth frequently. Reduce to simmer. When all froth has been skimmed off, add bay leaf, thyme, salt, and pepper. Reduce stock by simmering over very low heat for 2 to 3 hours.
3. Carefully strain stock through fine sieve lined with linen or muslin cloth.

Note: Stock may be kept in refrigerator in a tightly closed plastic container for about a week or 2, or it may be frozen. (Freezing the stock in ice cube trays and then storing the cubes in a freezer bag will allow you to use just the proper amount of stock whenever a recipe calls for it.)

Makes 8 cups

Fish Stock

Onion   ½ cup grated
Mushroom stems and parings   1½ cups
Small parsley bouquet   1
Lemon thyme sprig   1
Bay leaf   ½
Fish heads and bones (of white fish)   4 pounds
Dry sauvignon blanc   6 cups
Cold water   8 cups
Salt   ¾ teaspoon
Lemon juice   ¼ teaspoon

1. Place onion, mushrooms, parsley, thyme, and bay leaf in bottom of stockpot. Cover with fish heads and bones.
2. Cover with wine and water, season with salt, and add lemon juice. Bring to a boil, skimming frequently. Simmer gently, uncovered, for 2 hours. Strain through a muslin bag or sieve.

Variation: Prepare as above, but use only 4 cups red wine and 6 cups water. Bring to boil, skim, cover, and simmer for ½ hour. Strain liquid.

Makes 6 to 8 cups

Basic Cooked Fish

Fish is naturally tender and should never be overcooked; overcooking toughens it, dries it out, spoils the flavor, and may even give it an off-taste. The more often you cook fish, the better sense you will have about when your fish is "just right." The best rule for cooking fish comes from the Fisheries Association of British Columbia. It is so simple and effective that no one has as yet improved on it.

Measure fish at thickest part, including stuffing if used. For each inch of thickness cook at high heat:
10 minutes—if fresh or fully thawed
12-15 minutes—if partially thawed
20 minutes—if solidly frozen
Anticipate longer cooking time if fish is cooked in foil. (Fish can be cooked from frozen state. If necessary to thaw partially in order to portion, or to thaw fully to marinate, bread, or stuff, thaw in refrigerator in original wrappings.) When fish is cooked just right, it will separate into solid, moist sections when firmly prodded with a fork. Serve fish with melted butter, freshly squeezed lemon juice, and any of a number of different sauces.

Dan Ripley's Basic Poached Fish Fillets

Water   enough to fill ⅔ saucepan
Bay leaf   1
Black peppercorns   10 to 12
Lemon juice   2 tablespoons
Dry white wine   1 cup
Large garlic clove   1, unpeeled
Fish fillets (or whole small fish)   2

1. Select a large, deep saucepan (match to length of fillets) with a tight-fitting cover. Fill pan ⅔ full with cold water, or at least up to 1½ times deepest thickness of fish.
2. Add all ingredients except fish and bring poaching liquid to boil; simmer for 10 minutes.
3. Have fish ready—trimmed, rinsed, and dried (if necessary), or rolled (sole/flounder). Carefully place fillets in poaching pan. Return pan to bare simmer over high heat with cover on, but do not leave unattended. Check frequently and adjust burner temperature to maintain a bare simmer for 10 minutes per inch of fish thickness. Adjust cooking times for different sizes of fish.
4. Remove fillets with long, flat turner to toweling to drain quickly (and thoroughly) to prevent fish from cooling too much.

Note: Have all accompanying vegetables and sauces ready and hot. Properly poached fish should not be held under warm cover, but served immediately.

Serves 2 to 4

Basic Steamed Fish

Every season our commercial fishermen bring home a number of odd and uncommon fish which they have netted as an incidental catch. There is no commercial market for this fish, so it's given to friends or relatives. Most of this fish is so fresh it's still flopping, making it a prime candidate for steaming. Be sure to serve fish cheeks to your favorite person—they're the best part. Sinclair Philip of Sooke also likes to eat the steamed eyes: they're flavorless and tough like chewing gum.

Small white fish, firm-fleshed*   1 to 1½ pounds, cleaned
Coarse salt   2 teaspoons
Dry sherry or rice wine   2 tablespoons
Light soy sauce**   3 tablespoons
Sesame oil   1 tablespoon
Scallions   2, shredded lengthwise
Gingerroot   4 thin slices, shredded
Water   2 cups (or more, as needed)

1. Clean and scale fish. Do not remove head and tail. Score fish at 1½- to 2-inch intervals. Cut to, but not through, center bone.
2. Place fish on a platter. Sprinkle with salt and sherry. Let stand 10 minutes.
3. Sprinkle with soy sauce and sesame oil; then place shredded scallions and ginger on top of fish.
4. Place 2 inches of water in a large roasting pan. Place 2 soup bowls (or clean bricks) upside down in the water. Bring water to boil and carefully lower platter with fish onto top of bowls. Cover roasting pan and steam fish for 10 minutes over high heat.
5. Remove cover carefully, taking care to avoid hot steam. Use a plate lifter or 2 potholders to remove platter from steamer. Place platter on top of another platter of equal or larger size. Serve fish immediately.
6. Remove fish in sections, working from tail to head. Lift up backbone and break near head. Serve bottom half.

* We never use an oily fish for this recipe.
** Koon Chun is a good brand of light soy sauce. Whatever brand you buy, you should try to find one that says "thin" on the label.

Serves 4

Dan Ripley's Sautéed Bottom Fish—The Basic Technique

This is a basic recipe that works well for a number of different fish types: large fillets of impeccably fresh sole and flounder, greenlings, and even rockfish. Ask your fishmonger for the freshest variety of the day. Allow 6 to 8 ounces per person. You may ask the fishmonger to remove the bone line present in most of these varieties. This will make eating the fish much more pleasant, and you'll lose only about an ounce per fillet.

Large rockfish, cod, ocean perch, or flounder fillets   2
Freshly ground white pepper   to taste
Flour   1 cup (or more, as needed)
Unsalted butter (see Index)   4 tablespoons clarified

1. Trim and clean fillets. If necessary, rinse under cold running water, drain, and gently pat dry with paper towels. (Dan feels that any fish which has been out of the water for more than 24 hours should be rinsed.)
2. Keep fish cold until just before cooking. It may be removed from the refrigerator 5 to 10 minutes before cooking.
3. Sprinkle fillets with a bit of freshly ground white pepper. Salt is not necessary, especially if it is included in the sauce.
4. Dredge fillets lightly in flour and shake off excess.
5. Heat clarified butter in a sauté pan large enough to accommodate fish. You will need at least 2 tablespoons of butter per fillet. (Don't use too much, though, or you'll "boil" the fish in butter.)
6. Place fish "rough" side down in pan. Sauté until golden brown, then turn to other side. Sauté until visible flesh turns opaque, or until juices emerging from already cooked side begin to look somewhat opaque. Do not overcook! All fish should be just "cooked through."

Note: Do not try to sauté too much fish in one pan. If cooking for 4, it is far better to use 2 pans, one each for 2 fillets. Nor can you properly sauté fish for a crowd—the fish will not hold well under a cover (as many cookbooks suggest). Better to use small portions of fish as an appetizer if you're serving many people.

Serves 2

Basic Cooked Crab

First method:
(Cleaning crab before cooking)

1. Remove back of crab by forcing front edge of shell against solid object (bucket rim, oar blade, gunwale, shovel blade, etc.) and pulling down.
2. Break crab in two by folding shell up and down.
3. Remove viscera, but save for crab bisque or stock.
4. Pull off gill filaments. Discard.
5. Cook as soon as possible after cleaning: use 3 to 5 ounces of salt per gallon of fresh water (or use clean seawater). Bring to a boil, add crab, and boil for 15 minutes after water returns to boil. Remove crabs from kettle and immediately chill in ice or iced water.

Second method:
(Cooking crab before cleaning)

1. Bring salt water to boil, add crab backside down (the legs will fold over the belly as the crab dies instantly in the hot water). Cook for about 20 minutes after water returns to boil.
2. Place crab in iced water as soon as it is removed from pot.
3. When thoroughly chilled, raise and break off tail (triangular flap beneath belly). Break off back; wash out and discard insides, leaving clean white meat.
4. Break crab body in half and separate legs from body. Crack legs. Eat directly from shell or reserve meat for later use.

Warren's Easy Roast

Here is Warren Dimmick's foolproof way of cooking a perfect roast every time.

Eye of round roast   One, 4 to 5 pounds
Salt, pepper, and herbs   to taste

Rub roast with salt, pepper, and herbs. Place in 450° oven for 30 minutes. Turn off oven. Leave roast in oven to cook slowly for 1 hour. Remove from oven and let rest for 15 minutes before carving.

Serves 8 to 10

Sushi Rice

Three factors spell success or failure in the proper making of sushi: the rice, the quality of the topping, and the skill in handmaking the sushi pillows. Mastery of the latter is achieved only after long training or practice (rice pillows formed by a sushi master will have all the grains point in one direction—just try and see how difficult this seemingly simple task is). But everyone can do a fair job of selecting and cutting the topping and turning out good sushi rice.

Raw short-grain rice   1 cup
Cold water   1 cup, plus 2 tablespoons
Vinegar Mixture   as needed
Wasabi   garnish
Soy sauce   garnish

1. Wash rice in running water until water runs clear; drain in fine-holed colander or sieve for 1 hour.
2. Place rice in a pot with a close-fitting lid, add water, cover, and bring to a boil over high heat for 2 minutes. Reduce heat to medium (transfer to another burner preheated to medium if using an electric stove) and boil for another 5 minutes.
3. Over low heat, cook for 15 minutes or until all water has been absorbed (this is the critical stage where you can burn the rice—a low hiss from the lid will tell you when water is gone; listen closely, but do not open lid).
4. Turn heat up for just 20 to 30 seconds to dry off rice. Remove pot from heat; take off lid and spread clean kitchen towel over top of pot, replace lid, and let stand for 10 to 15 minutes.
5. Make Vinegar Mixture while rice is cooking.
6. Empty rice into wooden bowl or other nonmetallic tub and spread it evenly over bottom with wooden spatula. Run spatula through rice in right-and-left slicing motions to separate grains with 1 hand and use other hand to fan rice with large fan. (If you have problems doing both operations at once, have a helper fan rice.) Slowly add Vinegar Mixture as you toss rice. This is a critical point: if you add too much vinegar, the rice will be soggy, if you add too little, it will not stick. The rice should come out glossy and somewhat sticky.
7. Continue fanning and mixing until rice reaches room temperature, about 10 minutes. (You may not need all of Vinegar Mixture.) Keep rice in tub until ready to use; cover with clean cloth. Do not refrigerate or it will become mushy.
8. You are now ready to form rice into sushi pillows (have a bowl of cold water handy—the rice will stick to your hands unless they are very wet) and to top pillows with sliced seafood, meat, or even vegetables: let your imagination be your guide. Serve wasabi and soy sauce for dipping on the side.

Serves 3 to 4

Vinegar Mixture

Rice vinegar (do not use wine vinegar—it's too acidic)   ¼ cup
Sugar   ⅛ cup
Salt   ⅛ teaspoon

Combine ingredients in small saucepan. Stirring with a wooden spoon, cook over low heat until sugar and salt have dissolved. Remove from heat and set pot into a bowl with ice water (and ice cubes) to cool rapidly.

A Fresh Note

All the herbs and produce in the following recipes are meant to be garden fresh and the quantities are given accordingly. If you *must* use dried herbs, be sure to adjust the amounts. Additionally, these recipes will often refer you to the Index for instructions on how to make such commonly used ingredients as cream cheese, butter, mayonnaise, fish or chicken stock, etc.

Remember, you will achieve *best* results with these recipes if you go that extra step and make the effort to use the freshest ingredients.

Appetizers

Asparagus Pâté with Watercress Sauce

This is a recipe from the renowned Sooke Harbour House on southern Vancouver Island. At Sooke the vegetables called for in the dish are grown in the inn garden and are picked just before being used in the kitchen. Accompany this dish with a crisp northwest chardonnay, a dry riesling, or a fruity sauvignon blanc.

Asparagus tips　1 pound, steamed
Medium dill pickle　1, diced
Freshly ground black pepper　to taste
Phyllo pastry　4 sheets, halved lengthwise, wrapped in plastic until ready to use
Shallots　1 teaspoon finely chopped
Dry white wine　½ cup
Whipping cream　1½ cups
Watercress　1 small bunch, washed well and chopped; reserve 4 sprigs for garnish
Unsalted butter (see Index)　¼ cup

1. Drain asparagus and puree with pickle in a food processor or blender. Season with pepper.
2. Divide mixture into 4 portions. Layer 2 phyllo sheet halves and fold lengthwise into a long narrow strip. Place ¼ of filling at one end, leaving ½ inch clear at either edge, and roll gently toward center. At this point, fold in edges and continue rolling up to the end, until you have a neatly rolled asparagus pâté. Place in dry cloth and refrigerate. Repeat until remaining sheets are completed.
3. Add shallots to wine over high heat and reduce until syrupy. Add cream and again reduce until thick and creamy. Add watercress, stir well, and cook gently for a few minutes. Puree mixture in a blender. Season with pepper if desired. Keep warm.
4. Preheat oven to 425°. In a skillet with a metal handle, melt butter over high heat. Place pâtés, seam side up, in butter and, once they are evenly browned, turn over and pop into oven for approximately 4 minutes.
5. Remove from oven; pour sauce on serving plates and place 1 pâté in middle of each and garnish with reserved watercress.

Note:　The pâtés can be made ahead to the point where they are covered with a dry cloth and refrigerated.

Serves 4

Kelp Pickles

This recipe is an old northwest standby. And it is truly unique to our region. It calls for fresh bull kelp, Nereocystis, *which floats offshore, forming large groves in the upper subtidal region in areas with rocky bottoms. Bull kelp is best collected from boats, but you can occasionally find fresh plants on the beach, just after severe storms have torn them loose and driven them ashore. (Do not use dead or decomposing kelp for this recipe.)*

Bull kelp stems   4 cups peeled and sliced into rings or rectangular strips
Mixed pickling spice   1 tablespoon
Whole cloves   1 teaspoon
White wine vinegar   ¾ cup
Sugar   2½ cups

1. Soak kelp in fresh water for 3 days, changing the water several times a day to leech out the bitter-tasting salts.
2. Place spices in a cheesecloth bag, tie firmly, and simmer in vinegar and sugar for 5 minutes. Remove spices and pour hot syrup over the sliced kelp. Let stand overnight.
3. Next drain off syrup, heat to boiling, and pour over kelp again. Let stand overnight.
4. The next day, remove syrup and heat to boiling. Place kelp slices in hot jars, cover with boiling syrup, and seal. Or store pickles in a covered crock.

Makes 7 cups

Gravlax (Gravad Lax or Lox)

By whatever name this tasty fish is known, it is basically fresh, salt-and-dill-pickled salmon. Its taste and the delicate quality of its flesh depend on its freshness: the fresher the fish, the better the final product. It is simply not possible to make good Gravlax from fish that has been mishandled or is too old. Accompany Gravlax with a well-chilled premium lager, a bone-dry chardonnay or sparkling wine, or good iced Skagit River moonshine.

Whole salmon   1 to 3½ pounds
Coarse (kosher) salt   3 tablespoons
Sugar   3 tablespoons
White peppercorns   2 tablespoons crushed
Dill   1 large bunch
Mustard Dill Sauce   (optional)

1. Cut salmon into 2 long fillets. Bone carefully (remove small bones with tweezers).
2. Combine salt, sugar, and peppercorns. Rub half spice mixture over 1 salmon fillet side (flesh up) and place fish skin side down in deep glass or porcelain baking dish. Spread dill over fish. Rub other fillet with remaining spice mixture and place skin side up on first fillet.
3. Cover with heavy plastic wrap; set a platter slightly larger than the fish on top and a weight on top of the platter (cheeses, cans of food, or whatever). Refrigerate 48 hours. Turn fish over

every 12 hours, separating fillets slightly to baste with pan liquid.

4. When ready to serve, gently scrape seasoning off fish, remove fillets from marinade, and pat dry with paper towels. Place skin side down on cutting board. Slice thinly on the diagonal (you'll need an extrasharp knife!), detaching each slice from skin (do *not* cut through skin). Serve cold with crackers as an appetizer, on a bagel with cream cheese, or with Mustard Dill Sauce.

Note: After the flesh has been sliced from the salmon skin, the skin may be cut into narrow strips and dropped into very hot oil to cook until crisp. Serve the crisped skin with the Gravlax, or wrap it in sushi rice. The Gravlax is also good served on a sushi pillow with a dab of wasabi.

Serves 6 to 9

Mustard Dill Sauce

Dijon-style mustard   ¼ cup
Vinegar   2 tablespoons
Capers   1 teaspoon crushed
Dry mustard   1 teaspoon
Freeze-dried green peppercorns   1 teaspoon crushed
Olive oil   ⅓ cup
Dill   4 tablespoons chopped

1. Combine Dijon-style mustard, vinegar, capers, dry mustard, and peppercorns; slowly beat in oil until mixture thickens. Fold in dill. Chill for several hours before serving to let flavor develop fully.

Makes about ¾ cup

Matt Gudmundson's Pickled Salmon

This is an excellent recipe. It was given to me—with Matt's permission—by Carole Teshima of Bellingham.

Salmon   enough to fill 2-quart jar
Salt   as needed
Onions   thinly sliced, as needed
Sugar   ½ cup
Water   ½ cup
White vinegar   1½ cups
Pickling spices   4 heaping tablespoons

1. Split fish and remove backbone. Crosscut into 3- to 4-inch pieces. Salt heavily (a layer of fish, a layer of salt, etc.) and let sit for 24 hours.
2. Wash fish thoroughly in cold, running water.
3. Lay pieces skin side down and crosscut into ¼-inch-thick slices by cutting down and across between skin and meat.
4. Pack snugly, but not too tightly into jars with alternating layers of thinly sliced onions.
5. Combine sugar, water, vinegar, and pickling spices; bring to boil, chill, strain, and pour over salmon packed into jars.
6. After salmon has been covered with liquid, close jars tightly and refrigerate. Salmon will be ready to eat in a few days (but it will be much better in a few months).

Makes 2 quarts

Ahousat Smoked Salmon

This recipe was collected from the Ahousat, a small tribe of the West Coast people living on the rugged outer coast of Vancouver Island. Preservation of foods by woodsmoke is very popular among many peoples, but hard smoked salmon appears to be indigenous to the Northwest Coast. Woodsmoke possesses valuable drying and sterilizing properties.

Whole Salmon   1
Salt   as needed

1. Remove head by cutting across back of salmon from gill to gill.
2. Do not scale fish.
3. To open salmon, cut back along both sides of backbone. (Do not cut through the belly! According to legend, the salmon must be cut down the back or the year's salmon run will stop.)
4. Pull backbone away from meat and remove insides. Open fish flat.
5. Cut ¼-inch slices from fish in areas where meat is thickest, i.e., midway between outer edge and backbone area. Do not cut through skin. Take 1 or 2 slices about 6 inches long and 2 inches wide from each side of salmon. This helps meat to dry evenly and prevents spoilage in thicker areas. (Some people completely remove thin meat slices, while others keep them

attached at the tail.)

6. Leave a thick strip of meat, about ½-inch wide, all along outer edge of the fish. Three sharpened cedar sticks, about the thickness of a pencil, are placed across fish to hold it open. The ends of sticks are embedded in thick outer rim of meat. Work quickly, as fish tends to fall apart if exposed to air too long.
7. Hang fish by tail in smokehouse. To do this, push cedar stick through flat part of fish at base of tail. Let it hang in the center of cedar stick, which should rest on 2 poles of smokehouse rack.
8. Half-smoked salmon needs to be smoked for 1 to 3 days; fully smoked salmon may require 4 or more days. (In the past, fish was pounded several times a day during the smoking period to make it soft. Any small bones left in meat were also removed.) When smoking has been completed, sprinkle salt on meat and store for future use.
9. Before serving, soak overnight; then steam fish for 20 minutes.

Note: You should expect at least an 18 to 25 percent weight loss in your salmon after it is smoked.

Serves 4 to 6

Kid-Stuffed Mushrooms

This is my favorite recipe for using leftover kid (uncooked trimmings from roasts, et al.), but it also works very well with ground lamb. Though I feel it comes out best with large meadow mushrooms, you may also use smaller commercial mushrooms: just double or triple the number of mushrooms. You may in fact use tiny button mushrooms, remove the stems, and plop in dabs of filling. Accompany this with a Yakima Valley merlot or lemberger.

Ground kid   1 pound
Prepared horseradish   3 teaspoons
Chives   1 teaspoon chopped
Rosemary leaves   ½ to 1 teaspoon chopped
Garlic cloves   4, finely minced
Salt and freshly ground black pepper   to taste
Tabasco sauce or hot paprika   dash
Mushrooms   12 to 18
Dry sauvignon blanc   ⅔ cup
Unsalted butter (see Index)   ½ cup
White wine vinegar   1 tablespoon

1. Mix together kid, horseradish, chives, rosemary, garlic, salt, pepper, and Tabasco. Remove stems from mushrooms; stuff caps with filling.
2. Place in shallow baking dish. Combine wine, butter, and vinegar in saucepan over medium heat and pour over mushrooms.
3. Bake in 350° oven for 20 minutes; then quickly brown meat under broiler.

Serves 6 to 8

Lamb Balls

I usually buy my lamb whole, from a Lopez Island lamb grower, and I usually have a lot of odds and ends left to turn into ground lamb. Ground lamb can be turned into meat patties (just like your ordinary hamburger meat), but I like spicing it up a bit. Here's an easy party snack (accompany it with a good lager beer, ale, or red wine).

Ground lamb   2 pounds
Capers or pickled nasturtium buds   2 teaspoons
Prepared horseradish   2 teaspoons
Onion or green onion   2 tablespoons chopped
Chives   1 teaspoon finely minced
Garlic cloves   6, finely minced
Thyme   1 tablespoon
Salt and freshly ground black pepper   to taste
Tabasco sauce or Chinese chili sauce   1 teaspoon
Dry sauvignon blanc   1 cup
Unsalted butter (see Index)   1 cup
Shallots   2 tablespoons finely chopped
White wine vinegar   1 tablespoon

1. Combine first 9 ingredients into tiny (½-inch) meatballs and place in shallow 9- by 13½- by 1½-inch glass baking dish.
2. In heavy skillet combine wine and butter over low heat. When bubbling, add shallots; cook until shallots are transparent. Stir in vinegar and pour over meatballs.
3. Cook meatballs in 350° oven until they are barely done (still pink on inside), about 10 to 20 minutes. Remove from sauce and quickly brown under broiler. Serve hot.

Serves 8 to 12

Raw Beef Sushi

This is a fairly recent innovation which became popular after the Japanese discovered the taste of beef. While the Japanese version calls for specially raised Kobe beef, this sushi works beautifully with the tender and flavorful beef raised in the Pacific Northwest. It may take a bit of courage for you to eat raw beef, but be brave—just remember, your ancestors once lived in caves and ate raw meat. Accompany this dish with a hearty ale or stout.

Sushi rice (see Index)   as needed
Wasabi   as needed
Large garlic clove   1, sliced paper-thin
Raw beef slices   12, cut paper-thin (partially freeze beef to make cutting easier)
Soy sauce   as needed

To assemble: Form sushi pillows. With finger, spread thin layer of wasabi on top of rice. Place 2 or 3 slices garlic on top of wasabi. Top with slice of beef and serve immediately. Serve with wasabi and soy sauce for dipping on the side.

Serves 6 to 8

Kibbeh Sushi

This is a somewhat esoteric version of a standard Middle Eastern dish, but it is very tasty and wholesome. Accompany it with a hearty ale, porter, or stout.

Raw, twice-ground lamb   ¼ cup
Capers or pickled nasturtium buds   1 teaspoon mashed
Onion or green onion   2 teaspoons finely minced
Chives   ½ teaspoon finely sliced
Chervil or parsley   2 teaspoons finely minced
Salt and freshly ground black pepper   to taste
Sushi rice (see Index)   as needed
Nori seaweed*   3 sheets, quartered into lengthwise strips and toasted
Wasabi   as needed
Elephant garlic clove   1, thinly sliced
Quail egg yolks   12
Japanese soy sauce   as needed

1. To make Kibbeh, combine lamb, capers, onion, chives, and chervil. Season with salt and pepper to taste.
2. Form 12 sushi pillows (the "pillows" are small, mounded balls of sushi rice), wrap with toasted nori strip, leaving a low (¼-inch) lip at the top to hold kibbeh. Place a dab of wasabi and a couple of slices of garlic on each pillow.
3. Equally divide kibbeh among sushi pillows. Top each portion with a quail egg yolk. Serve immediately with wasabi and soy sauce on the side for dipping.

* To toast the nori strips, hold them over a hot burner until they turn green and crisp. Be careful not to burn them, for they will taste horrid if you do.

Serves 4 to 6

Escargots with Hazelnut Butter

The Shelburne is a restaurant in a lovely old inn out on Washington's Long Beach peninsula, in a place where one would not expect a first-rate restaurant. But owners Tony and Ann Kischner and chefs Eric Jenkins and Cheryl Walker have a knack for finding the area's best produce, meat, fish, and shellfish. A dinner I had at the Shelburne in late fall of 1983 was one of the best I have ever had anywhere. The escargots were particularly noteworthy. They are petit gris snails gathered locally in the gardens of the Long Beach peninsula, and shucked, cleaned, and precooked at the inn. They are amazingly superior to the canned snails commonly used in our restaurants. I liked them so much, I asked for the recipe, et voilà!

Snails   48, cooked
Dry white wine   ½ cup
Cognac   1 tablespoon
Thyme   1 teaspoon
Bay leaves   2
Unsalted butter (see Index)   1½ pounds
Shallots   3, finely minced
Garlic cloves   2, finely minced
Hazelnuts   ½ cup finely chopped
Parsley   ½ cup finely chopped

1. Marinate snails in wine, cognac, thyme, and bay leaves at least 4 hours, refrigerated. Whip together all remaining ingredients until well blended; refrigerate.
2. Heat escargot serving dish. Sauté 6 snails per serving with 6 tablespoons hazelnut butter over medium heat until foaming. Serve immediately with plenty of fresh french bread.

Serves 6 to 8

Red Turban Snails in Herb Butter

The red turban is a large (one to two inches across), cone-shaped marine snail common on rocks from the intertidal zone down to about sixteen fathoms. It is very good to eat and quite easy to collect. Make sure you only gather live snails—those that withdraw into their shells when disturbed and close the opening with their limy operculum/trapdoors. A bone-dry sauvignon blanc, chardonnay, or riesling goes well with these snails, or try a sparkling wine from Hinzerling Vineyards in Washington or Château Benoit in Oregon.

Oyster or shiitake mushrooms   2 cups sliced
Shallots   2 tablespoons chopped
Turban snails*   36, cooked and drained
Unsalted butter (see Index)   ¼ cup
Cream   ½ cup
Thyme   1 teaspoon finely chopped
Small bay leaf   1
Nuoc mam   ½ teaspoon
Freshly ground black pepper   ⅛ teaspoon
Madeira wine   ½ cup

1. In saucepan, cook mushrooms, shallots, and snails in butter until shallots are tender.
2. Stir in cream, thyme, bay leaf, nuoc mam, and pepper. Simmer, uncovered, for 10 minutes. Remove bay leaf.
3. Add madeira; heat through. Serve in individual snail dishes.

* Scrub snails well. Boil in large kettle of water for 20 minutes. Drain; carefully pull at operculum. Snail should come out with operculum. If not, carefully twist snail from body with toothpick. Remove operculum; wash off intestines and dark gall bladder with cold water.

Serves 6 to 8

Leafy Hornmouth Snails with Sea Urchin Butter

I first enjoyed this dish at a lovely New Year's dinner at the Sooke Harbour House on southern Vancouver Island. Red turban snails and other snails may be substituted for the leafy hornmouth. If you substitute the Oregon triton snail, check each snail after cooking to be sure the bilious pouch is not broken. Otherwise a bitter flavor invades the meat (Sinclair Philip's note).

Hornmouth snails   40
Water   4 cups
Oil   2 tablespoons
Vinegar   ½ cup
Dry white wine   1 cup
Sea urchin roe   ¼ cup (rinse and discard black strands)
Unsalted butter (see Index)   ¾ cup, room temperature
Shallots   1½ tablespoons finely chopped
Parsley   1½ tablespoons finely chopped
Celery   1 tablespoon minced

1. Soak snails in fresh water for 1½ hours. Change water and resoak for 2 hours.
2. Boil sea snails for approximately 3 minutes from boiling point in a solution of water flavored with oil, vinegar, and white wine. (The oil will facilitate removal of snail from shell.) Drain and cool.
3. When cool, remove meat from snail with pin or crab pick and cut off horny operculum. Remove as much of animal as possible. If snail cannot be removed, cover shell with towel and break with a hammer. Remove meat from broken shell; pick over for shell fragments. All parts of the snail except the black bilious pouch are edible. The bile of the leafy hornmouth is quite mild; that of the Oregon triton snail is quite bitter. Cut saved fragments of snails into small chunks, rinse briefly in diluted vinegar and reserve for stuffing.
4. Scrub, clean, and boil whole snail shells from which meat has successfully been removed for 20 minutes. Reserve for stuffing.
5. In a mortar or bowl, pound together the sea urchin roe, butter, shallots, parsley, and celery until well mixed and of an even orange color. If light orange, add more roe until mixture is a clearly defined orange color.
6. Preheat oven to 400°. Mix sea snail meat with roe butter so that snail particles are well distributed. Stuff snail shells, place in oven-proof dish, and heat briefly, until butter begins to melt. Place any remaining stuffing in a small oven-proof porcelain dish and put into oven at same time as snails. (There's no sense in freezing the remaining mixture, since sea urchin roe becomes bitter and loses its fruitiness when frozen.)
7. Remove from oven when butter has melted. Serve hot.

Serves 8

Marinated Mussels

This dish works very well with the coarser mussels that grow on exposed rocks (collect only when there's no red tide warning); but the more tender, delicately flavored cultured mussels may be used as well.

Medium-sized mussels in their shells   48
Dry sauvignon blanc   1 cup
Light soy sauce   1 cup
Sugar   1 teaspoon
Cayenne pepper   ½ teaspoon
Black peppercorns   12
Gingerroot   ½ tablespoon minced

1. Wash and scrub mussels well and cut off the byssus threads ("beard"). In a big 6-quart pot, set the mussels into ½-inch deep water and bring to a boil over medium heat. Cover pot and steam mussels for 2 minutes or until they just open. Do *not* overcook. Discard any mussels that do not open.
2. Drain water immediately; reserve ½ cup. Remove and discard top half of each mussel shell. In a glass or porcelain mixing bowl, combine wine, soy sauce, sugar, cayenne, peppercorns, ginger, and the mussel broth. Stir until sugar is dissolved.
3. Arrange mussels in 8-inch-square glass cake pan, pour sauce over them, and seal pan with heavy-duty plastic wrap (do *not* use aluminum foil!). Let marinate in refrigerator for a minimum of 24 hours.

Serves 4

Fried Clams on the Half Shell

This is a quick and easy appetizer made with one of our great natural resources, fresh clams. These clams go well with almost any dry white wine, but I prefer them with a northwest sauvignon blanc or semillon, or even with a good northwest porter (like Blackhook Porter—or even Russian Imperial Stout).

Littleneck or Manila clams   48
Medium eggs   2, lightly beaten
Flour, seasoned with salt and pepper to taste   as needed
Unsalted butter (see Index)   ½ cup (or more, as needed)
Hot paprika   to taste
Chervil or parsley   2 tablespoons finely chopped
Salmon caviar   1- to 2-ounce jar, drained (optional)

1. Scrub whole clam shells well; open clams with clam knife. Cut clam from top shell but leave attached to bottom shell. Discard top shell. Thoroughly clean clam by rinsing (save pea crabs!). Drain on paper towels.
2. Dip clams, shell up, first in egg, then in seasoned flour.
3. Place clams in hot butter in heavy iron skillet, shell on top. (Depending on the size of your skillet, the clams and the butter may have to be divided into several batches.) Fry until brown. Sprinkle with paprika and chervil and serve hot. (Optional: top with salmon caviar.)

Note: Pea crabs are tiny soft-shell crabs that are often found inside larger clams. They are delicious, so if you happen upon 1 or more, be sure to eat them whole or use them as garnish.

Serves 4 to 6 as a snack, 12 to 14 as an appetizer

Oysters in Cider Vinegar Butter

Sinclair Philip, who serves this dish at the Sooke Harbour House on Vancouver Island, says that this recipe was inspired by a recipe from Bon Appetit *magazine called "Huîtres au Beurre du Vinaigre du Cidre." This dish calls for an excellent northwest sparkling wine, like the superb brut made at Château Benoit by wine maker Rich Cushman.*

Oysters*   6 unshucked
Dry apple cider   ¼ cup
Cider vinegar   2 tablespoons
Fish stock (see Index)   ¼ cup
Small shallot   1, minced
Leek   2 tablespoons minced, white portion only
Dried seaweed (alaria, if possible)   ½ tablespoon
Whipping cream   2 tablespoons
Unsalted butter (see Index)   ⅓ cup cut into ½-inch cubes, refrigerated
Chives   garnish

1. Shuck oysters over bowl to catch liquor. Place oysters in small bowl. Reserve deep half of shell for serving.
2. Transfer oyster liquor to saucepan; add cider, vinegar, stock, shallot, leek, and seaweed; bring to boil. Poach oysters in liquid, 1 minute on each side, depending on thickness. Remove and keep warm.
3. Warm shells by placing in pan of hot water; cover.
4. Add cream to pan liquids; bring to boil and reduce by half (about 4 minutes) until thick.
5. Immediately whisk in butter pieces. Remove warm oyster shells from pan; dry and arrange for serving.
6. Reheat oysters in sauce; then place on half shells and pour sauce over each oyster. Sprinkle with chives and serve immediately.

* The oyster shells called for in the recipe may be substituted with puff pastry shells.

Serves 2

Oysters with Oyster Mushrooms

Here is another dish for anyone who does not like to eat oysters raw. The delicate flavor of oysters fresh from the water goes very well with the equally delicate flavor of oyster mushrooms. Accompany this dish with a light, fruity, bone-dry Oregon riesling.

Oyster mushrooms   ½ cup sliced
Shallots   2 tablespoons chopped
Leeks   2 tablespoons chopped, white portion only
Dijon or Düsseldorf mustard   1 teaspoon
Hot paprika   pinch
Unsalted butter (see Index)   6 tablespoons
Flour   6 tablespoons
Nuoc mam   ½ teaspoon
Cream   1½ cups
Medium egg yolks   2, beaten
Dry sherry   4 tablespoons
Small Pacific oysters   24
Rock salt to hold oysters in baking pan   as needed

1. In saucepan, cook mushrooms, shallots, leeks, mustard, and paprika in butter until shallots are tender but not browned. Make a roux by carefully blending in flour. Stir in nuoc mam and cream. Cook, stirring constantly, until thick and bubbly.
2. Gradually add sauce to egg yolks, beating constantly with wire whisk to blend. Return to saucepan; cook for 1 more minute. Stir in sherry. Remove pan from burner, place lid on it, and place saucepan in larger pan filled with hot water to keep warm.
3. Shuck oysters. Keep oysters in lower shell. Place shells on rock salt in shallow baking dish. Bake in 350° oven for 5 minutes. Spoon about 1 tablespoon sauce over each oyster. Bake 5 minutes longer.

Makes 12 to 24 appetizers

Creamed Oysters

East Coast foodists like to put down the West Coast's Pacific oyster as inferior in taste to the marshy, flavorless oyster of the East Coast. This assertion is far from true. The taste of our oysters varies with their place of origin, and our best oysters surpass the much-vaunted eastern oysters in flavor and delicacy. But some oysters come from muddy estuaries—which mean their flavor is not as fine as it could be—and they do not always reach the market in perfectly fresh condition. In that case they may be cooked before they are eaten. The trick to properly cooking an oyster is to do as little as possible to it. Never overcook it! Accompany this dish with a fruity eastern Washington muscat wine.

Extrasmall Pacific oysters   1 pint, shucked
Unsalted butter (see Index)   ½ cup
Flour   ½ cup
Cream   2 cups
Hot paprika   ¼ teaspoon
Freshly ground sea salt and white pepper   to taste
Dry sherry   ½ cup
Toast

1. Simmer oysters for 3 minutes in their liquor or until the edges begin to curl.
2. Melt butter in top of double boiler; gently blend in flour with wire whisk. Add cream, stirring all the time, and cook until thickened.
3. Add oysters, sprinkle with paprika, and season with salt and pepper to taste.
4. When oysters are heated through, add sherry, blending slowly so sauce will not curdle. Serve over toast.

Serves 4 to 6

Oyster and Mushroom Pie

This pie may be served in small slices as an appetizer or it can make a good lunchtime main course. Accompany it with a well-chilled, thirst-quenching lager beer.

Small onion   1, chopped
Oysters   1 quart, shucked and chopped
Unsalted butter (see Index)   4 tablespoons
Cracker Crumb Piecrust (unbaked)
Eggs   3, well beaten
Cream   ½ cup
Mushrooms   ½ cup finely chopped
Oyster liquor (from sauté pan)   ½ cup
Oyster sauce   2 teaspoons

1. Sauté onion and oysters in butter for about 3 minutes; remove with a slotted spoon and spread evenly over bottom of pie crust.
2. Mix eggs, cream, mushrooms, oyster liquor, and oyster sauce; pour over oysters and bake at 325° for 50 minutes.

Serves 6 to 8

Cracker Crumb Piecrust

This crust may, of course, be used for other pies, with the addition of sugar for sweet fruit and other dessert pies. (Mix crumbs with ½ cup sugar before adding butter.)

Cracker crumbs 1½ cups
Unsalted butter (see Index), or lard for a better crust ½ cup

1. Measure crumbs into a medium-sized bowl. Melt butter and slowly pour over crumbs while stirring with a fork.
2. Pour crumb mixture into 8- or 9-inch pie plate. Press it firmly against sides and bottom of pan with back of a large spoon (or with a well-greased hand). Another pie plate may be fitted down into the crumbs to help shape crust.
3. Rest piecrust by chilling in refrigerator for 1 hour or longer.
4. Preheat oven to 400°.
5. Remove crust from refrigerator; carefully fit a piece of heavy aluminum foil over crust to prevent scorching. Do not weigh down crust.
6. Bake on middle shelf of oven for 5 minutes. Watch carefully to make sure edges and bottom do not burn. Lift foil and check progress after 3 minutes. Remove crust from oven. Place on rack to cool before filling. It will harden as it cools.

Note: To make a stronger flavored crust, sauté 1 finely chopped small onion in butter as it heats. When onions are transparent, proceed as below, pouring butter (with the sautéed onion) on the crumbs, etc.

Makes one 8- or 9-inch shell

Calamari Piccata

The quality of this dish depends on the quality and tenderness of the squid. At the Shelburne Inn, where we first encountered this spicy squid, all ingredients are, of course, at their best. Try to get very small and very fresh squid from your fishmonger for this dish.

Red onion   1, julienned
Unsalted butter (see Index)   ½ cup, melted and clarified
Squid body (cut into rings) and tentacles   1½ pounds
Capers   ½ cup, plus some of marinade in which it is bottled
Dry white wine   1 cup
Lemon juice   ¾ cup
Tomato   1, diced
Parsley   ½ cup chopped
Salt and freshly ground black pepper   to taste
Unsalted butter (see Index)   ½ cup

1. Sauté onion in clarified ½ cup butter until transparent. Add squid pieces; sauté about 2 minutes. Add capers and marinade, wine, lemon juice, tomato, parsley; cook about 2 minutes more.
2. Remove squid to warmed serving plate.
3. Reduce sauce about 2 minutes more. Season to taste. Add ½ cup butter and stir until melted. Pour sauce over squid and serve immediately.

Serves 6 to 8

Marinated Squid

Here's another dish introduced to the Northwest by fishermen of Mediterranean origin. I first enjoyed it in the company of some Yugoslav fishermen. It was accompanied by copious amounts of freshly baked bread and homemade red wine.

Squid   2 pounds
Baking soda   2 tablespoons
Cold water   4 gallons
Boiling salted water   1 gallon
Freshly ground black pepper   to taste
Olive oil   ¼ cup
Lemon juice   ⅓ cup
Mint   1 teaspoon chopped
Parsley and chervil   1 tablespoon chopped
Garlic cloves   6, minced (or more, according to your personal preference)
Chicory or radicchio lettuce (inner leaves)   garnish
Tomato cubes   garnish
Lemon wedges   garnish

1. Clean squid. Rinse and drain mantle on paper towels; cut into ½-inch squares or into ¼-inch strips. Chop tentacles into ¼- to ½-inch pieces.
2. Soak in baking soda/water solution for 2 to 4 hours. Remove, rinse well.
3. Drop squid pieces into boiling salted water; reduce heat, simmer for 3 to 5 minutes, depending on toughness of fresh squid, until tender. Check as you cook. Do not overcook or squid will toughen.
4. Combine pepper, oil, lemon juice, mint, parsley, and garlic and pour over squid. Marinate in refrigerator for several hours. Serve on bed of lettuce leaves. Garnish with tomato and lemon.

Serves 6 to 8

Deep-Fried Squid

This dish was introduced to the Northwest by Mediterranean fishermen who make good use of the "strange" creatures incidentally caught in their nets. You may accompany the squid with a dry white wine (sauvignon blanc, semillon), but it would be more authentic to drink a simple generic red or perhaps a light lemberger.

Squid   2 pounds
Lemon juice   2 tablespoons
Salt   ½ teaspoon
Freshly ground white pepper   ⅛ teaspoon
Milk   2 tablespoons
Medium egg   1, beaten
Flour   1 cup
Vegetable oil   for deep-frying
Lemon wedges   garnish

1. Clean squid and wash well. Separate mantle from tentacles and cut mantle into ½-inch-wide rings. Sprinkle tentacles and rings with lemon juice, salt, and pepper.
2. Combine milk and egg by beating slightly.
3. Dip squid into milk/egg mixture and roll in flour.
4. Heat oil to 350° and deep-fry squid until lightly browned (about 3 to 5 minutes). Drain on paper towels; serve with lemon wedges.

Serves 6 to 8

Sautéed Crawfish

You'll probably need to catch your own crawfish for this dish, for these tasty "miniature lobsters" must be very fresh. But it's well worth the effort. Enjoy this dish with a chilled Oregon chardonnay.

Raw crawfish tails in shell   4 to 5 cups cleaned
Shiitake or oyster mushrooms   3 cups sliced
Green onions   ½ cup sliced
Olive oil*   ½ cup
Salt and freshly ground black pepper   to taste
Basil   2 tablespoons finely chopped
Oregon chardonnay   ½ cup

1. Sauté crawfish tails, mushrooms, and onions in oil over medium-high heat until crawfish tails begin to change color. Drain off half of oil. Sprinkle with salt and pepper and chopped basil.
2. Add chardonnay; cook over high heat until tails have turned bright red and meat is opaque. Serve hot.

* You can use ¼ cup olive oil and ¼ cup melted clarified butter in place of the ½ cup olive oil.

Note: You clean crawfish just as you would prawns by pulling shell segments off the meat.

Serves 10 to 12

Sea Urchin Rinse

Sea urchin roe is one of those odd, but eminently tasty foods that has been enjoyed in Europe and the Orient seemingly forever, but that has been appreciated in our region for only a short time. It is good that sea urchin is finally coming into its own in the Pacific Northwest, for our sea urchins are exceptionally tasty. Most neophytes first experience sea urchin roe as uni *on their sushi, but Sinclair Philip at the Sooke Harbour House on Vancouver Island serves it in a variety of ways. He prefers eating it raw, however, fresh from the water.*

Sinclair collects a number of sea urchins, removes and cleans their roes, and then fills a large sea urchin shell whose top has been sliced off brimful with the roe. It is a most interesting method of serving this marine delicacy, for sea urchin spines move for a long time after the animal has been killed, and his filled sea urchin shells have been known to "crawl" over food displays.

Sinclair suggests the following method for rinsing sea urchin roe:
    When eating sea urchin roe raw, try rinsing it in *dry* pear cider for about 15 seconds before serving. It helps to reinforce its fruitiness.

Allow 2 to 4 sea urchins per serving

Giant Barnacles

These are the largest of the West Coast barnacles, regularly growing to two or three inches in diameter and four to five inches in height. A beaklike protuberance projects above the edge of the shell. Barnacles are rather peculiar crustaceans, because they have no hearts or circulatory systems, but they do have tasty pink depressor muscles inside their shells and they carry delicately flavored roe in their mantle cavities. These are the edible parts; the rest of the animal is discarded. But this still leaves you with a lot of meat from a four-or five-inch barnacle. The meat tastes like a cross between scallop and crab (though really with a flavor of its own). Anyone wanting a steady supply of these must dive for the hard-shelled tasty creatures. Accompany with a lightly flowery dry riesling and eat without condiments to get the full pleasure of their delicate flavor.

Giant barnacles   2 to 4 per serving (depending on size)
Salt   to taste
Water

1. Boil barnacles for 15 to 20 minutes in salted water.
2. Remove from water; cool. Pull off beak/trapdoor; remove legs and upper body. Carefully spoon out roe. Rinse shell and remove pink muscle meat.

Scattered East-West Sushi

The molluscs and crustaceans in this recipe may be replaced with other shellfish, or with raw cubed fish. Or, if you're averse to eating raw seafood, the clams, shrimp, and squid may be lightly cooked—just until they turn opaque. (Do not overcook.) Do not use oysters, since their flavor does not go well with vinegared rice. Accompany this dish with a good well-chilled lager beer.

Sushi rice (see Index)   3 cups
Button mushrooms   12 to 24 (depending on size)
Raw (preferably *live* shrimp; use cooked shrimp if fresh is not available)   ½ cup
Raw squid mantle   ½ cup cubed
Raw geoduck belly meat (or cooked crab)   ¾ cup cut into ¼-inch cubes
Mild cheese (Northwest Jack or mild Pleasant Valley Gouda)   ½ cup diced
Japanese or English cucumber   ½ cup cut into ¼-inch cubes
Mixed sprouts (mung, pea, adzuki, lentil)   1 cup
Salmon caviar   2 ounces, drained
Snow peas   12, parboiled in salted water and refreshed in cold water
Squid tentacles   12, trimmed to ½- to ¾-inch lengths and sautéed in butter until they open up
   like flowers; attached at head ring
Soy sauce   ¼ cup
Wasabi   1 tablespoon

1. Toss sushi rice with mushrooms, shrimp, squid mantle, geoduck, cheese, cucumber, and mixed sprouts and lightly pack onto a plate, mounding it in the shape of a cone.
2. Make a shallow, craterlike depression on top, fill with salmon caviar (caviar may spill over side of crater like "lava"). Arrange snow peas vertically along base of cone. Place squid tentacle rings decoratively along base of cone, 1 squid "flower" between each 2 snow peas. Serve soy sauce and wasabi on the side.

Serves 6 to 8

Caviar-Topped Cherry Tomatoes Stuffed with Seasoned Cream Cheese

I simply love good fresh sturgeon caviar and I love to eat it straight from the container or perhaps on some sour cream-covered toasted lefse. But not everyone likes caviar right from the start. Here's a tasty way of introducing the caviar neophyte to this great delicacy. Accompany this dish with a bone-dry chardonnay or northwest sparkling wine.

Ripe cherry tomatoes   12
Seasoned Cream Cheese   about 12 teaspoons
Columbia River sturgeon caviar   1 to 2 ounces

Hollow out cherry tomatoes; fill cavity ⅘ full with Seasoned Cream Cheese. Top with caviar. Serve chilled.

Makes 12

Seasoned Cream Cheese

Cream cheese (see Index)   1 pint
Green onions   6, white and green portions
Small garlic cloves   2, chopped
Capers or pickled nasturtium buds   2 teaspoons drained

Process all ingredients in blender or food processor until very smooth. Refrigerate until ready to use.

Makes 1 pint

Salmon Caviar Mold

This is a great dish for a festive occasion and it should be accompanied with a great northwest chardonnay or with one of the excellent dry sparkling wines made by Hinzerling in Washington and Château Benoit in Oregon.

Unflavored gelatin 1 envelope
Cold water ¼ cup
Sour cream (see Index) 1¾ cups
Mayonnaise (see Index) 2 tablespoons
Lemon juice 2 tablespoons
Onion 2 teaspoons grated
Hot paprika 1 teaspoon
Salmon or steelhead caviar 4 ounces, drained
Salt and freshly ground white pepper to taste
Parsley sprigs garnish
Lemon wedges garnish
Toast rounds or toasted lefse triangles

1. Sprinkle gelatin on water and let stand until softened.
2. Warm 1 cup sour cream over low heat, add gelatin/water mixture, and stir constantly until gelatin melts, 1 to 2 minutes.
3. Remove from heat and add mayonnaise, lemon juice, onion, and paprika, blending well. Remove and set aside 1 tablespoon salmon caviar. Fold remaining caviar into sour cream mixture. Stir gently so berries do not break. Season to taste with salt (if necessary—the salmon caviar may be quite salty) and white pepper.
4. Turn mixture into buttered 2-cup mold and chill until firm (about 3 to 4 hours). Unmold on serving plate. Spread ¾ cup sour cream over caviar mold. Sprinkle reserved salmon caviar on top. Surround mold with parsley sprigs, lemon wedges, toast rounds, and toasted lefse triangles.

Serves 8 to 10

Salmon Caviar Paté

This is a very special dish, and it calls for the best and firmest salmon caviar available, the luscious chum salmon caviar from Cossack Caviar in Seattle. Serve with thinly sliced pumpernickel and a chilled, dry sauvignon blanc.

Unflavored gelatin   1½ teaspoons (½ envelope)
Cold water   2 tablespoons
Salmon caviar   4 ounces, drained
Sour cream (see Index)   ¾ cup
Red onion   ¼ cup finely chopped
Parsley   3 tablespoons finely chopped
Tabasco sauce   6 drops
Heavy cream   ¾ cup, whipped

1. Sprinkle gelatin over water in small bowl to soften 3 minutes.
2. Set bowl in simmering water until gelatin is completely dissolved, about 3 minutes.
3. Reserve 2 tablespoons caviar for garnish. Combine remaining caviar with sour cream, onion, parsley, and Tabasco sauce in large bowl.
4. Stir in gelatin.
5. Fold in whipped cream.
6. Turn into an oiled 2½- to 3-cup mold. Chill until firm, about 3 hours.
7. Unmold onto serving plate; garnish with reserved caviar.

Makes 3 cups

Captain Whidbey Cheese Balls

Here's an old party favorite with a regional touch. They also make great holiday gifts. Serve with homemade crackers and with a bottle of good cabernet sauvignon or merlot.

Oregon blue cheese   one 5-pound wheel
Unsalted butter (see Index)   5 pounds
Walnuts   1 cup chopped
Chives   1 cup finely chopped
Garlic   2 teaspoons finely chopped
Freshly ground white pepper   1 teaspoon

1. Soften cheese and butter at room temperature. Blend well.
2. Add walnuts, chives, garlic, and pepper.
3. Roll into ¾-pound balls. Refrigerate. The balls may be rolled in additional chopped walnuts before serving (use an additional cup of chopped walnuts).

Makes 12 to 15

Blue Cheese-Stuffed Eggs

The somewhat smoky taste of ripe Oregon blue cheese goes very well with full-flavored duck eggs.

Duck eggs   6, hard-cooked
Oregon blue cheese   ¼ cup crumbled
Mayonnaise (see Index)   2 tablespoons
Whipping cream   2 tablespoons
Chervil or parsley   1 tablespoon minced
Chives   ½ teaspoon finely chopped
Nuoc mam   ¼ teaspoon
Freshly ground black pepper   ⅛ teaspoon
Lovage   ¼ teaspoon very finely chopped
White tarragon wine vinegar   1 tablespoon
Golden whitefish caviar   2 ounces drained

1. Cut eggs in halves and remove yolks. Mash yolks with all remaining ingredients, except caviar.
2. Fill egg whites with mixture. Chill until ready to serve. Just before serving top each filling with a dab of caviar.

Serves 6 to 8

Soups

Scallop Chowder

This chowder is also very good when made with cubed geoduck belly meat or with chopped steamers or butter clams. Serve it with a crisp chardonnay and freshly baked crusty french bread.

Salt pork   ½ cup diced
Onions   2, chopped
Potatoes   2, diced
Pink swimming scallops (whole if small; quartered if large)   1 pint
Milk   1 quart
Salt and freshly ground white pepper   to taste

1. Sauté pork cubes and remove them; sauté onion in pork grease.
2. Boil potatoes until almost tender, about 15 to 20 minutes, then drain.
3. Add scallops to onions; sauté until they are almost opaque. Add remaining ingredients and bring to simmer but do not boil. Simmer gently for 5 minutes. Season with salt and pepper to taste.

Serves 4

Northwest Winter Solstice Seafood Bisque

This recipe was developed by Bob Meade for his Le Cuisinier cooking school above Chuckanut Bay to celebrate the sinking and reemergence of the sun at the winter solstice of 1982. Serve with chilled northwest champagne, chardonnay, or with a full-bodied, dry Oregon riesling.

Whitefish fillets (rockfish or cod)   2 pounds
Fish stock (see Index) or clam juice   6 cups
Clams   1 pound, minced, juices reserved
Shrimp   ½ pound, cooked
Salt and freshly ground black pepper   to taste
Cayenne   ⅛ teaspoon
Cream   1½ cups
Orange   6 very thin slices

1. Carefully bone fillets (or have your fishmonger bone them). Simmer them in stock until they flake easily.
2. Add clams with their juices and cooked shrimp. Cook an additional 2 minutes. Season with salt, pepper, and cayenne.
3. Puree all in a food mill or food processor until very smooth.
4. Add cream and reheat. The bisque should be very thick at this point. If a thinner bisque is desired, add more cream.
5. Reheat, but do not boil. Serve very hot with an orange slice at the side of the bowl. (Bob sees the orange slice as a reminder that the sun has reached the southernmost point of its course and is now on the way back to us.)

Serves 6 to 8

Clam Chowder

Salt pork   2 tablespoons diced
Onion   ½ cup chopped
Potatoes   1 cup diced
Clam nectar   2 cups
Clams   1 pint
Heavy cream   2 cups
Unsalted butter (see Index)   3 tablespoons
Salt   to taste
Freshly ground white pepper   ¼ teaspoon

1. Sauté pork until crisp; remove pieces from pan and reserve for use later as a garnish.
2. Add onion to hot pork fat, and sauté until tender and transparent, but not brown.
3. Combine sautéed onion and diced potatoes in a deep saucepan with the clam nectar and gently simmer for about 15 minutes, or until the potatoes are cooked.
4. Stir in clams and remaining ingredients, and heat until hot throughout, but do not boil.

Serves 6

Oyster and Oyster Mushroom Chowder

Oysters have long been popular in the Pacific Northwest; the delicately flavored oyster mushrooms are becoming increasingly popular—and available. Accompany this dish with a dry white wine or with a good lager beer or pale ale.

Small oysters   1 quart shucked
Oyster liquor   1 cup
Unsalted butter (see Index)   3 tablespoons
Flour   1 tablespoon
Cream   2 cups
Shallots   2, finely chopped
Chervil or parsley sprig   1, finely chopped
Nuoc mam or light soy sauce   ½ teaspoon or
     Salt   to taste
Freshly ground white pepper   to taste
Oyster mushrooms   ½ pound

1. Heat oysters in their liquor to just below boiling point (until their edges curl). Drain, saving liquor.
2. Melt 1 tablespoon butter and blend in flour to make a roux; add cream gradually, stirring constantly. Bring to boiling point and cook 1 minute. (Make sure it does not burn!)
3. Add shallots, chervil, nuoc mam, and pepper.
4. Add cleaned mushrooms and oyster liquor to cream sauce. Swirl in remaining 2 tablespoons butter. Blend. Serve hot.

Serves 6

Oyster Chowder

This is a tasty and nourishing luncheon dish. Make sure to use only freshly shucked oysters or you won't enjoy the flavor as much. Accompany with a premium porter.

Oysters   1 quart shucked
Lovage   ½ cup finely sliced
Celery   ¼ cup chopped
Potatoes   2 cups diced
Nuoc mam or light soy sauce   1 teaspoon or
   Salt   to taste
Freshly ground white pepper   to taste
Boiling water, fish stock (see Index), or clam nectar   1 cup
Egg yolks   2, well beaten
Cream   1 cup

1. Drain oysters, reserving the liquor, and coarsely chop.
2. Arrange alternate layers of lovage and celery, potatoes and oysters in a heavy cast-iron pot. Season with nuoc mam and pepper.
3. Add water and oyster liquor; simmer for ½ hour or until potatoes are tender.
4. Mix yolks with cream and add to chowder.
5. Heat to just below boiling point for only a few minutes and serve piping hot. Do not overcook after adding egg, or chowder will curdle.

Serves 4 to 6

Michael's Café Mussel Chowder

This is a favorite at Michael's Café in Coupeville (and, according to Michael Anter, a never-before shared recipe). The home cook can serve this to a large crowd or reduce the quantities—the recipe serves forty (it's great for summer get-togethers). Serve with a dry riesling, chardonnay, semillon, or sauvignon blanc.

Mussels   15 pounds (scrubbed and bearded)
Bay leaves   3
Parsley   1 bunch, finely chopped
Dry white wine   2 cups
Olive oil   ½ cup
Garlic cloves   3 ounces, finely chopped
Shallots   4 ounces, finely chopped
Celery   2 bunches, chopped
Large firm tomatoes   4, chopped
Water   1½ gallons
Large yellow onions   8, chopped
Green onions   3 bunches, chopped
New potatoes   10 pounds, diced
Unsalted butter (see Index)   2 cups, clarified
Flour   4 cups
Cream   1 quart
Maggi Liquid Seasoning   8 ounces
Salt and freshly ground black pepper   ½ tablespoon each, or to taste

1. In a large (40-quart) stockpot, combine mussels, 2 bay leaves, parsley, wine, olive oil, garlic, shallots, 1 bunch celery, and tomatoes. Cover pot and cook on high heat until steam escapes the lid, approximately 10 minutes.
2. Open lid and stir once or twice, bringing mussels at bottom of pot up to top to insure uniform cooking. When all shells are open, remove from heat and drain of all liquid (Michael's comment here: Be sure to save this wonderful nectar!).
3. In another large stockpot (40-quart), add all of mussel poaching nectar and 1½ gallons of water. Bring to a boil and add other bunch of chopped celery, chopped onions, green onions, and remaining bay leaf. Bring to a boil again and continue cooking for 10 minutes.
4. Add potatoes. Cook for 15 minutes longer, then reduce heat to low and hold.
5. Make a roux with clarified butter and flour. Gradually add roux to chowder base to thicken.
6. Add mussel meat, cream, Maggi, and salt and pepper to taste. Stir well and serve.

Serves 40

Abalone and Mushroom Soup

Fresh abalone are hard to find these days (humans have literally eaten these tasty snails off the rocks), but you may substitute large limpets in this recipe; just use three or four times the amount, unless you discover a large clump of extra-large keyhole limpets. This dish goes very well with any dry white wine (or even a blanc de noir) or with a good lager beer or well-chilled pale ale.

Shiitake mushrooms   4
Celery stalks   4
Smoked country ham slices   2
Small abalone feet (the flat part the snail crawls on)   4
Lean pork   2 ounces
Cornstarch   1 teaspoon
Light soy sauce   1 tablespoon
Vegetable oil   1 tablespoon plus ½ teaspoon
Freshly ground black pepper   ½ teaspoon
Gingerroot   2 slices
Salt   ½ teaspoon
Boiling water   6 cups

1. Slice mushrooms and celery. Cut ham and abalone into matchsticks. Set aside.
2. Cut pork into very thin slices; mix with cornstarch, soy sauce, 1 tablespoon oil, and pepper.
3. Heat ½ teaspoon oil in heavy pot; fry ginger and salt for ½ minute. Then pour in water. Return water to boil; add mushrooms and pork mixture.
4. Simmer, covered, for 10 minutes. Add ham and abalone; simmer for an additional 5 minutes and serve.

Serves 6 to 8

Lettuce and Fish Soup

The pleasant bitterness of chicory goes very well with the sweetness of fresh whitefish. The chicory may be replaced with similar salad greens: endive, fresh young dandelion greens, shepherd's purse, lamb's-quarters, et al., or a combination of garden and wild greens may be used. This soup is enhanced by a nicely dry, crisp sauvignon blanc, semillon, or a premium pale ale.

Cabezon or other firm white fish   ¼ pound, chunked
Cornstarch   1 teaspoon
Lemon juice   2 teaspoons
Nuoc mam   2 teaspoons
Dark soy sauce   1 tablespoon
Freshly ground white pepper   ½ teaspoon
Vegetable oil   1 tablespoon
Chicory lettuce   1 head
Water   6 cups
Nasturtium leaves   garnish
Sour cream (see Index)   3 to 4 tablespoons
Salmon caviar   6 to 8 teaspoons drained
Large capers   6 to 8

1. Toss fish with cornstarch to coat. Mix lemon juice, nuoc mam, soy sauce, pepper, and oil and marinate fish in this mixture. Separate and wash chicory leaves.
2. Bring water to a boil. Toss in chicory. Simmer, covered, for 5 minutes; add fish mixture and simmer 5 to 8 minutes more.
3. Serve hot. Top each serving with a nasturtium leaf. Place a dollop of sour cream on each leaf; top sour cream with about ½ teaspoon salmon caviar. Place 1 large caper atop each mound of salmon caviar.

Serves 6

Hot and Sour Fish Chowder

This recipe is a modification of a Chinese cold-weather soup designed to warm both body and soul. Different kinds of white-fleshed fish may be substituted for the cabezon and the type and amount of hot pepper may be adjusted to fit your personal tolerance level of oral heat. The soup may be prepared several hours ahead of time and reheated just before it is served. Accompany it with hot mulled wine or a good stout or porter.

Cabezon   ½ pound, cut into 1-inch chunks
Dry sherry, marsala, or madeira   ½ tablespoon
Lemon juice   1 teaspoon
Cornstarch   ½ teaspoon
Vegetable oil   1 tablespoon
Leeks   1 cup coarsely chopped
Chicken or fish stock (see Index)   3 cups
Tender heart of cattail stalks   ½ cup finely cut
Soft tofu   one 3-inch square, diced
Nuoc mam   1 teaspoon
Light soy sauce   1 tablespoon
White wine or rice vinegar   2 tablespoons
Freshly ground white pepper and finely ground black pepper   ⅛ teaspoon each
Red pepper (hot paprika, cayenne, or crushed chilies)   ⅛ to 2 teaspoons (depending on
    taste preference and tolerance)
Cornstarch   2 tablespoons
Sauvignon blanc   3 tablespoons
Medium egg   1, beaten
Sesame oil   1 teaspoon
Fresh coriander (cilantro)   1 tablespoon chopped
Sour cream or crème fraîche (see Index)   6 to 8 tablespoons
Salmon caviar   6 to 8 teaspoons drained
Lemon wedges   garnish

1. In a bowl, mix fish with sherry, lemon juice, and ½ teaspoon cornstarch.
2. Heat oil in large saucepan (I use a Chinese sandy pot) over medium heat until almost smoking; add leeks and stir until they turn soft. Pour in stock and bring to a boil. Add fish, stirring gently to keep pieces apart, then drop in cattail hearts. Return to boil and let boil for 2 minutes. Gently drop in tofu (making sure not to break the pieces); season with nuoc mam and soy sauce; return to boil.
3. Stir in vinegar, peppers, and 2 tablespoons cornstarch dissolved in sauvignon blanc. Stir constantly until soup thickens.
4. Turn off heat, stir in egg, and wait a few seconds until egg is set; then pour soup into individual serving bowls. Sprinkle with sesame oil and coriander.
5. Drop a large dollop of sour cream onto each bowl. Top with salmon caviar. Serve lemon wedges on the side.

Serves 6 to 8

Shrimp Stew

This stew is tastiest when made with freshly caught shrimp, cooked on the beach, and rushed home to the stew kettle. But it works with high-quality flash-frozen shrimp as well. Accompany it with a dry riesling, sauvignon blanc, or chardonnay.

Large onion   1, finely minced
Medium garlic clove   ½
Unsalted butter (see Index)   4 tablespoons
Flour   4 tablespoons
Prepared mustard   ½ teaspoon
Nuoc mam or salt   1 teaspoon
Freshly ground white pepper   ⅛ teaspoon
Shrimp   2 cups, cooked
Milk   2 cups
Rich whipping cream*   1 cup
Parsley   1 tablespoon minced
Paprika   to taste

1. Cook onion and garlic in butter until onion is tender.
2. Remove garlic and add flour, mustard, nuoc mam, and pepper to the butter. Stir to blend. When thoroughly blended, add shrimp, milk, and cream, stirring constantly until stew begins to thicken. Heat thoroughly.
3. Add parsley; sprinkle with paprika after placing in individual serving bowls.

* Some whipping creams are richer than others. I like to let mine sit a short while at room temperature, then skim the surface for the richest cream.

Serves 4 to 6

Island Oyster Stew

This is a favorite dish of the residents of Vancouver Island's sheltered east coast, where sumptuous oysters grow on the tideflats of secluded inlets and where cattle produce a rich milk from the tasty dryland grasses.

Oysters   1 pint shucked
Salt and freshly ground white pepper   dash
Heavy cream   2 cups
Milk   2 cups
Worcestershire sauce   1 tablespoon
Unsalted butter (see Index)   6 tablespoons
Paprika   garnish (optional)
Parsley   garnish (optional)
Salmon caviar   garnish (optional)

1. Cook oysters in oyster liquor until edges curl, about 3 minutes.
2. Season with salt and pepper.
3. Add cream and milk and gently heat almost to boiling point, but do not boil (use double boiler if necessary).
4. Add Worcestershire sauce and remove stew from heat.
5. Add butter, and garnish with either paprika and parsley, or with salmon caviar (1 teaspoon per bowl).

Serves 6

Oyster and Tofu Soup

This soup appeared somewhat strange to me when I first tried it in a Chinese restaurant—but it is surprisingly tasty. I have since tried several versions of this. Here's my favorite (accompany it with a first-rate lager beer like Henry Weinhard's Private Reserve).

Small oysters   2 cups shucked
Scallions   2, halved and slightly crushed
Lemon juice   1 teaspoon
Dry sherry   1 tablespoon
Cornstarch   1 tablespoon
Vegetable oil   ½ tablespoon
Chinese sour mustard greens   ⅓ cup thinly slivered
Chicken stock (see Index)   3 cups
Soft tofu   one 3-inch square, diced
Nuoc mam   ½ teaspoon
Freshly ground white pepper   pinch
Hot paprika   ¼ teaspoon

1. Marinate oysters with scallions, lemon juice, sherry, and cornstarch for 10 minutes. Then discard scallions.
2. Heat oil in heavy saucepan or wok over medium heat (I like to use a large Chinese sandy pot), add sour mustard greens, and stir for 1 minute. Pour in stock and bring to boil. Add oysters, tofu, nuoc mam, pepper, and paprika. Heat to a full boil and immediately remove from heat. Serve hot.

Serves 4 to 6

Crawly Critter Soup

This is the kind of soup where a lot of substitution is possible, as long as you adhere to the proper quantities. You may use shrimp, mantis shrimp, gooseneck barnacle stalk meat, giant barnacle muscle, large or small crabs, crawfish, etc. Accompany with freshly baked country bread or with whole wheat rolls and with a bone-dry chardonnay or riesling.

Unsalted butter (see Index)   4 tablespoons
Onions   2, finely chopped
Leeks   2, white portion only, finely chopped
Crawfish meat   1 pound
Shrimp or barnacle meat   ½ pound
Chicken stock (see Index)   4 to 6 cups (enough to cover meat)
Salt and freshly ground black pepper   to taste
Crab meat   1 pound
Nuoc mam   1 tablespoon
Lemon juice   1 tablespoon
Salmon or whitefish caviar   1 to 2 tablespoons (according to taste)
Cayenne pepper   dash
Chives   ¼ cup thinly sliced

1. Melt butter in a saucepan. Sauté onions and leeks until limp (about 5 minutes).
2. Add crawfish and shrimp meat; sauté without browning for an additional 5 minutes. Do not overcook.
3. Add stock, salt, and pepper. Heat to simmer. Add crab meat; stir well. Season with nuoc mam and lemon juice.
4. Carefully stir caviar into soup (make sure not to break berries). Add extra stock if soup is too thick. Simmer for 10 minutes. (Season with cayenne if you like a little bite.)
5. Pour into individual bowls. Sprinkle with chives.

Serves 6 to 8

Chicken Soup with Prawns and Quail Eggs

Some of the best commercially available prawns come from British Columbia—in both fresh and frozen forms. They are quite sweet and have a clean taste, without the annoying iodine undertaste too often found in processed shrimp. As an extra bonus, many of these prawns carry large quantities of bright orange roe underneath their tails. This roe, when present, should be carefully stripped off (proceed from the rear to the front, otherwise the tail appendages will resist removal of the roe) and added to the soup with the prawns. Accompany this dish with a very fruity dry riesling or gewürztraminer.

Chicken carcass   1, cut into large pieces
Small onion   1, ground
Small carrot   1, ground
Celery stalk   1, ground
Cold water   3 quarts
Bay leaf   1
Thyme   ¼ teaspoon chopped
Salt and freshly ground white pepper   to taste
Large prawn tails (preferably from British Columbia)   6 to 8
Lemon juice   from ½ lemon
Quail eggs   10
Parsley   1 tablespoon chopped
Prawn roe   (optional)

1. Put chicken pieces into large pot (I like to use a Chinese sandy pot, because of its even heat distribution). Add onion, carrot, and celery. Cover with water and bring to a boil over medium heat, frequently skimming froth off top.
2. Season with bay leaf, thyme, salt, and pepper. Use less salt and pepper than you normally would—the reduction will increase the potency of the spices. Reduce by simmering over very low heat for 2 to 3 hours.
3. Carefully strain broth through a sieve lined with a linen or muslin cloth.
4. Just before broth is finished, prepare prawns. Strip off roe (if present) and set aside. Plunge prawns into boiling water for a few seconds, until flesh is just turning opaque. Do not overcook, or prawns will toughen and become chewy. Remove from water and chill under cold running water. Add lemon juice.
5. Return broth to pot and bring to a boil over high heat. When broth is bubbling, quickly add quail eggs, one at a time (break shells carefully—they're quite thin), turn off heat, and let eggs poach.
6. When eggs are almost done, shell prawns, slice into ¼-inch slices, and add to soup. Sprinkle with parsley. Add roe, if available. Serve hot, making sure everyone gets an equal amount of prawn and roe.

Serves 8 to 10 as a dinner course; serves 4 to 5 as a luncheon soup

Tofu and Crab Meat Soup

Tofu has become increasingly popular during the last decade or so, and several types of this bland, versatile bean curd—which was once restricted to health food stores—are now available in supermarkets throughout the Northwest. Catch your own crab, or buy it fresh at the dock to assure maximum freshness and flavor. This is a good winter dish, since crab is at its best during the cold season. A crisp dry sauvignon blanc will enhance the flavors of this soup; so will chunks of crunchy, freshly baked french bread.

Dungeness or rock crab meat   6 ounces
Soft tofu   two 3-inch squares
Shiitake or oyster mushrooms   ½ cup sliced
Vegetable oil   1 tablespoon
Gingerroot   1 teaspoon minced
Chicken stock (see Index)   3 cups
Nuoc mam   1 teaspoon
Dry sherry   ½ tablespoon
Cornstarch   2 tablespoons
Sauvignon blanc   3 tablespoons
Freshly ground white pepper   pinch

1. Remove all cartilage from crab meat; rinse meat with cold water. Drain.
2. Cut tofu into ½-inch cubes. Dice mushrooms.
3. Heat oil in saucepan over medium heat and stir in ginger and crab meat; cook for 30 seconds. Add stock, nuoc mam, and sherry. Bring to a boil and drop in mushrooms and tofu.
4. Mix cornstarch and wine. Blend into soup when soup returns to boil. Stir until thickened and season with pepper.

Serves 4 to 6

Lummi Island Seafood Stew

This recipe can be adapted to many different types of fish and shellfish. For example, you may use small beach crabs, mantis shrimp, limpets, sea snails, or sea cucumbers. An herbaceous sauvignon blanc and hot garlic toast harmonize well with this stew.

Fish stock*   3 quarts
Clam nectar   4 cups
Flat lager beer   ¾ cup
Thick carrots   2, sliced diagonally
Celery stalks   4, sliced diagonally
Garlic cloves   6 to 12 (according to preference), crushed in a press
Leek   1, cut into ¼-inch slices
Hot paprika   1 teaspoon
Cornstarch   1 tablespoon
Dry sauvignon blanc   2 cups
Freshly ground white pepper   to taste
Nuoc mam   1 tablespoon
White wine vinegar   1 teaspoon
Live crawfish   12 (or more), well-scrubbed
Medium shrimp   12, unshelled
Live pink swimming scallops   12 to 24
Manila or littleneck clams   12 to 24 or
    Butter clams   12
Cabezon fillets or other firm whitefish   four, ½-inch thick (4 to 5 ounces each), cut
    into chunks

1. Strain stock into large kettle; discard heads and bones. Add clam nectar, beer, carrots, celery, garlic, leek, and paprika. Bring to a boil and simmer until carrots are crisp-tender.
2. Combine cornstarch with ½ cup wine and stir into simmering stew. Simmer 5 minutes, then add pepper, nuoc mam, and vinegar.
3. Bring to rolling boil and add crawfish. Split shrimp down back and remove sand vein. Add to stew together with scallops, clams, and fish chunks. Add remaining 1½ cups wine.
4. Return to boil and boil 5 to 10 minutes or until crawfish are bright red and clams and scallops have opened. Serve in large bowls with generous amounts of liquid.

* Make fish stock by simmering 2 pounds fish heads and bones of cabezon, greenling, rockfish, or other white-fleshed fish in 3 quarts water for about 2 hours. Add more water as needed.

Serves 6

Sea Urchin Soup

This very tasty soup with an odd ingredient, sea urchin roe, is a favorite at the Sooke Harbour House on Vancouver Island. The sea urchin must be very fresh, otherwise the roe loses its fruitiness and takes on a slightly bitter taste.

Unsalted butter (see Index)   1 tablespoon
Small shallot   1, minced
Tomato   ¼, finely diced
Sea urchin roe   ¾ cup cut up (discard parts of urchin other than orange roe)
Fish velouté*   2 cups
Gewürztraminer   2 tablespoons
Egg yolk   ½, lightly beaten
Whipping cream   1 tablespoon
Crème fraîche (see Index)   1 tablespoon
Sea urchin roe   1 teaspoon

1. Melt butter in medium-sized pan and sauté shallot and tomato over medium heat. Add roe, fish velouté, and wine, and, as you increase the heat, combine all ingredients well.
2. When soup is heated through and is ready to be served, blend together egg yolk and cream; add and stir well.
3. Pour soup into 2 bowls; divide crème fraîche topping between them and place on surface of soup; top with sea urchin roe (½ teaspoon each).

* To make fish velouté, thicken 2 cups of fish stock (see Index) with a roux made from 2 tablespoons unsalted butter (see Index) and 2 tablespoons flour (cooked together for 3 minutes).

Serves 2

Watercress and Nasturtium Soup

The watercress and nasturtium in this soup enhance each other's taste (they're closely related plants), adding a pleasant nuance to a very tasty dish. Try it with a fruity sauvignon blanc or semillon, or even with a big riesling.

Watercress leaves and stems   1 cup finely chopped
Zucchini   1 cup grated
Leeks   1 cup finely chopped, white portion only
Potatoes   1 cup peeled and chopped
Boston lettuce   ½ cup chopped
Chervil leaves and stems   ½ cup snipped
Green onion   ¼ cup sliced
Small garlic clove   1, crushed in press
Chicken stock (see Index)   2 cups
Nasturtium leaves and stems   1 cup finely chopped
Nuoc mam   ½ teaspoon
Freshly ground white pepper   to taste
Whipping cream   1 cup
Sour cream (see Index)   4 tablespoons
Chives   2 teaspoons finely cut
Salmon caviar   2 teaspoons drained

1. In large saucepan, combine first 9 ingredients. Simmer, covered, for 10 to 15 minutes until potatoes are tender.
2. Add nasturtiums. Stir. Pour soup into work bowl of food processor; process with steel blade until very fine. Strain through very fine sieve; set aside vegetables (see note below for suggested use of strained vegetables). Season to taste with nuoc mam and pepper. Add whipping cream; heat through—do not boil. Pour into individual bowls.
3. Combine sour cream and chives and spoon a dollop atop each bowl; top sour cream with ¼ teaspoon salmon caviar per serving.

Note: Mix strained vegetables from soup with ½ cup shredded Chinese cabbage, 1 teaspoon nuoc mam, 1 stalk fresh, finely chopped lemongrass, and 2 teaspoons toasted white sesame seeds; wrap servings of 1 to 2 tablespoons each in rice paper or won ton skins, deep fry them, and serve as a side dish with the soup.

Serves 4

Cream of Winter Kale and Apple Soup

Sinclair Philip, Pia Carroll, and the rest of the kitchen staff at the Sooke Harbour House firmly believe that most of the vegetables served at that remarkable inn should come from the kitchen garden—even in the depth of winter. Kale is one green that grows well on the Sooke bluffs year-round; it is tastiest after the first frost.

Unsalted butter (see Index)   ¼ cup
Garlic clove   1, minced
Onion   ⅓ cup finely diced
Curly or Siberian kale   6 cups washed and dried, thick stems discarded
Flour   ¼ cup
Chicken stock (see Index)   6 cups
Cooking apple   ½, cored, peeled, and thinly sliced
Thyme   pinch
Tarragon   1 teaspoon
Freshly ground black pepper   to taste
Crème fraîche (see Index) or whipped cream   garnish
Chives   garnish

1. In large saucepan, melt butter over low heat; add garlic and onion and sauté. Add kale; stir well and cover pan for a few minutes to soften leaves.
2. Stir in flour to form roux and let cook for a few minutes. Slowly stir in stock, apple, and seasonings and bring to a boil. Lower heat; let simmer for ½ hour. Correct seasoning. Let cool; then process in blender until smooth (can be made ahead to this point).
3. Heat soup over moderate flame; pour into warmed bowls; place a small dollop of crème fraîche plus a sprinkle of chives atop each. Serve.

Serves 6

Garden Cress and Leek Soup

Garden cress, also known as "pepper grass," grows very well in the Pacific Northwest. In mild winter areas, it will continue to grow throughout the cold season. It goes well with leeks, another one of our more prolific winter vegetables. Accompany this soup with a crisp gewürztraminer.

Leeks   2, white portion only, minced
Garden cress   1 bunch, chopped
Unsalted butter (see Index)   4 tablespoons
Medium potatoes   4, grated
Nuoc mam   1 teaspoon
Half-and-half   1 quart
Freshly ground white pepper   ¼ teaspoon
Egg yolk   1, beaten
Chervil or parsley   1 tablespoon finely chopped
Sour cream (see Index)   2 to 3 tablespoons
Salmon caviar   2 to 3 teaspoons drained
Lemon wedges   garnish

1. Sauté leeks and cress in butter over low heat for 5 minutes. Cook until leeks turn golden. Stir constantly; do not burn leeks.
2. Combine next 4 ingredients in a double boiler and simmer for about 20 minutes, until soup thickens. Stir in yolk and chervil just before serving. Top each serving with ½ teaspoon of sour cream; place ½ teaspoon salmon caviar atop cream. Serve with lemon wedges.

Serves 4 to 6

Bok Choy Soup

This is a delicate soup which nicely balances the flavor of lamb and bok choy. It's a perfect pick-me-up for a cool summer day. Accompany this soup with a big chardonnay or a light lemberger.

Lean lamb   2 ounces
Cornstarch   ½ teaspoon
Dark soy sauce   2 teaspoons
Freshly ground black pepper   ¼ teaspoon
Vegetable oil   1 teaspoon
Gingerroot   2 slices (about the size of a quarter each)
Boiling water   1½ quarts
Nuoc mam   1 tablespoon
Bok choy or sui choy   1 head, green part
Madeira wine   to taste

1. Slice lamb very fine and mix with cornstarch (coat well), soy sauce, pepper, and oil.
2. Heat a little oil in saucepan (just enough to grease bottom). Fry ginger for 30 seconds; add boiling water. Stir in nuoc mam.
3. Slice bok choy greens and add to boiling water. Cover pot and simmer vegetable for 10 minutes. Add lamb mixture. Cover pot and allow to simmer for 10 to 15 minutes more. Remove ginger. Just before serving, stir in Madeira wine. Serve hot.

Serves 10 to 12 if served as part of a formal dinner; serves 4 to 6 as a light lunch course

Broccoli Yogurt Soup

This is another one of those "all but the kitchen sink" recipes. The broccoli may be safely exchanged for such exotica as bracken fiddlenecks (well brushed), salmonberry shoots, hop shoots, watercress, sheep sorrel, or whatever combination of wild and tame greens catches your fancy. Don't worry: unlike wild meats, all are very easy to catch, even for an urban flatfoot.

Unsalted butter (see Index)   2 tablespoons
Olive oil   1 tablespoon
Garlic cloves   5 to 6 (or a dozen or more, just try and see how much you can take), finely chopped
Sweet onion of medium girth   1, chopped
Hot paprika   2 tablespoons
Chicken stock (see Index)   2 cups
Weedy sauvignon blanc   2 cups
Ripe tomatoes   1½ pounds, peeled, seeded, and coarsely chopped
Broccoli stems   1 cup finely chopped
Light soy sauce   ½ teaspoon
Nuoc mam   ¼ teaspoon to 1 tablespoon (depending on taste)
Freshly ground black pepper   ¼ teaspoon
Plain low-fat yogurt   2 cups
Pleasant Valley Gouda, farmer's cheese, or mild white Cheddar cheese   2 to 4 ounces, grated
Cilantro   garnish

1. Melt butter in large kettle and add oil. Mix. Add garlic and onion and sauté until lightly browned. Add paprika and sauté for 1 minute.
2. Add stock, wine, tomatoes, broccoli, soy sauce, nuoc mam, and pepper. Bring to boil, reduce heat, and simmer about 20 minutes.
3. Stir in yogurt very slowly and cook over low heat until just heated through (do not overheat or yogurt will separate into curds and whey).
4. Ladle into individual serving bowls and sprinkle with cheese and chopped cilantro.

Serves 4 to 6

Broccoli Goat Cheese Soup

This soup is best when made with fresh Skagit Valley broccoli and with the tangy Cascadian goat cheese from Briar Hills Dairy in Chehalis.

Broccoli stems   ½ pound, finely chopped
Water   1¾ cups
Sweet onion   2 tablespoons minced
Unsalted butter (see Index)   ¼ cup, melted
Flour   3 tablespoons
Cream   3½ cups
Milk   4 cups
Goat cheese   3¼ cups grated
Nuoc mam   ½ teaspoon
Freshly ground white pepper   to taste

1. Cook broccoli in water, approximately 3 to 5 minutes, until tender. Drain.
2. Cook onion in butter until transparent. Do not brown. Slowly stir in flour, making sure no lumps form. Add cream and milk and cook, stirring constantly, until smooth and thickened. Do not boil or cream may curdle.
3. Add cheese and broccoli and season with nuoc mam and pepper. Stir until cheese is melted. Serve hot.

Serves 8

Watercress Soup

Watercress grows wild and plentiful along northwest stream and lake shores. It's free for the taking—just make sure the water is not polluted.

Unsalted butter (see Index)   4 tablespoons
Onion   1, coarsely chopped
Lovage leaves   1 tablespoon chopped (optional)
Garlic clove   1, minced
Meadow mushrooms or commercial mushrooms   1 cup finely chopped
Lemon juice   from 1 lemon
Watercress leaves and tender upper stems   3 cups chopped
Chicken stock (see Index)   4 cups
Nuoc mam   ½ teaspoon
Freshly ground white pepper   to taste
Whipping cream   1 cup
Thin cucumber slices, cut into daisy or dahlia pattern   garnish
Salmon or golden whitefish caviar   1½ teaspoons drained

1. Melt 2 tablespoons butter in a large heavy pot and add the onions, lovage, and garlic. Cook, stirring frequently, for about 2 minutes. Add mushrooms and lemon juice; stir. Cover and cook over low heat for about 15 minutes.
2. Add watercress and stir; cook just until watercress wilts. Stir in stock. Simmer, uncovered, for about 10 minutes.
3. Puree mixture in food processor. Return to pot and slowly bring to boil. Swirl in remaining 2 tablespoons butter; season with nuoc mam and pepper; add cream and heat through. Pour into individual bowls. Float 1 cucumber "flower" on top of each bowl; garnish center of flower with caviar.

Serves 6

Buttermilk, Nasturtium, and Cucumber Soup

You can make this soup with peeled and seeded American cucumbers, but Japanese cucumbers (which are now widely grown by truck farmers throughout our region) have such a superior flavor that they are well worth searching out. There are also no bothersome seeds to worry about. If your garden does not produce a sufficient number of nasturtium leaves, use garden cress or watercress instead. Accompany this soup with a spicy gewürztraminer.

Japanese cucumbers 2, chunked
Nasturtium leaves 1 cup chopped
Chicken stock (see Index) 1 cup
Buttermilk 3 cups
Pickled nasturtium buds or capers 1 teaspoon
Dill 2 tablespoons chopped
Nuoc mam 1 teaspoon
Freshly ground white pepper to taste
Nasturtium flowers 4 to 6, washed to make sure no bugs hide inside tube

1. Place first 5 ingredients in a food processor (in batches if bowl is too small). Puree until smooth. Season with dill, nuoc mam, and pepper to taste.
2. Serve in glass bowls, well chilled. Float 1 nasturtium flower on top of each bowl.

Serves 4 to 6

Cold Cucumber Soup

Medium Japanese cucumber*   3 (or 4 small) or
    Large English cucumbers   2 or
    Medium American cucumbers   3
Unsalted butter (see Index)   2 tablespoons
Leek   1, minced white and green portions
Bay leaves   2
Flour   1 tablespoon
Chicken stock (see Index)   3 cups
Salt   to taste
Freshly ground white pepper   ⅛ teaspoon or to taste
Half-and-half   1 cup
Lemon juice   from ½ lemon
Dill sprig   1, chopped
Sour cream or créme fraîche (see Index)   6 teaspoons
Golden whitefish caviar   3 teaspoons

1. Slice 2 cucumbers (1½ English cucumbers)—peel if using American cucumber.
2. Melt butter, add sliced cucumber, leek, and bay leaves; cook slowly until tender. Do not brown.
3. Discard bay leaves. Add flour and mix in well (make sure no lumps form). Add stock, salt, and pepper and bring to boil. Reduce heat and simmer for 20 to 30 minutes, stirring occasionally.
4. Puree soup by pressing through a sieve (or puree in food processor) and chill in refrigerator for several hours.
5. Halve remaining cucumbers (peel and remove seeds if using American cucumbers) and grate. Add to soup with half-and-half, lemon juice, and chopped dill to taste.
6. Serve in chilled soup cups and top each serving with a dollop of sour cream and ½ teaspoon of golden whitefish caviar (do not use dyed whitefish or lumpfish caviar; they're horrid).

* You may use a standard American cucumber for this dish, but I much prefer using the long and slender Japanese *kyūri* cucumber whenever a recipe calls for cucumber, or the elongated English cucumber. Neither of these cucumbers has a waxed skin, and thus need not be peeled if you like a touch of green (and extra flavor) in your soup. If you use the squat American cucumber, you must peel it.

Serves 6

Purslane Soup

Purslane is generally thought of as a much-maligned garden weed, but it is actually a very tasty vegetable—not only raw, in salads, but also in soups which are enhanced by its crisp taste. This soup calls for a vin rosé, a light pinot noir, or a grenache or pale ale.

Pork (fat or lean—as you like it)   2 ounces, minced
Cornstarch   1 teaspoon
Freshly ground black pepper   ½ teaspoon
Light soy sauce   1 tablespoon
Vegetable oil   1 tablespoon
Water   6 cups
Nuoc mam   1 tablespoon
Lemon juice   2 teaspoons
Purslane leaves and tender stems   1 pound, coarsely chopped
Medium duck eggs or chicken eggs   2

1. Toss minced pork with cornstarch to coat, then mix with pepper, soy sauce, and vegetable oil.
2. Bring water to boil in heavy pan. Add nuoc mam and lemon juice; toss in purslane; cover pot and simmer 10 minutes. Add pork mixture. Boil, covered, for 5 minutes.
3. Beat eggs well and gently stir into soup. Serve as soon as eggs have set slightly.

Serves 6 to 8

Potato Soup

This is very much a standard potato soup with a surprise finish—salmon caviar. Somehow potatoes and salmon caviar seem to have an affinity for each other; try salmon caviar with other potato dishes as well! Accompany this dish with a chilled chardonnay, dry riesling, or first-rate lager beer.

Leeks   4, trimmed and cleaned
Unsalted butter (see Index)   4 tablespoons
Small garlic clove   1, finely minced
Medium onion   1, finely chopped
Water   4 cups
Chicken stock (see Index)   4 cups
Flour   2½ tablespoons
Nuoc mam   1 teaspoon
Freshly ground white pepper   to taste
Medium potatoes   4, quartered
Heavy whipping cream   1 cup
Half-and-half   2 cups
Chives   10 to 12 teaspoons chopped
Salmon caviar   10 to 12 tablespoons drained

1. Trim roots of leeks. Quarter leeks lengthwise, making sure not to cut all the way to the root end. Swirl leeks in cold water (like a brush) to remove all traces of sand and loam. Drain well; chop.
2. Melt 1 tablespoon butter in large kettle, add leeks, garlic, and onion, and cook until tender but not browned. Add water and stock and bring to boil.
3. Knead flour into remaining 3 tablespoons of butter to form a paste and stir into boiling mixture with a whisk to blend well (you may want to roll paste into little balls and stir them in one at a time). Season with nuoc mam and white pepper.
4. Add potatoes, reduce heat, and simmer until potatoes are soft. Press soup through sieve. Cool. Stir cream and half-and-half into soup; then chill. Just before serving, top each bowl of soup with a sprinkling of chopped chives and a generous dollop of salmon caviar.

Serves 10 to 12

Cold Potato and Oregon Blue Cheese Soup

This soup has only one cooked ingredient, the potatoes, and these should be cooked right before the soup is made to take full advantage of their delicate flavor. The amount of blue cheese called for in the recipe may be adjusted to conform to personal taste. I find that this soup goes very well with a Château Benoit brut sparkling wine.

Chinese cabbage (Napa cabbage)   2 cups coarsely shredded
Oregon blue cheese   1 tablespoon
Medium red potatoes   4, cooked, peeled, and quartered
Milk   2 cups
Nuoc mam   1 teaspoon
Freshly ground white pepper   ¼ teaspoon or to taste
Sour cream or crème fraîche (see Index)   4 teaspoons
Golden whitefish or steelhead caviar   2 teaspoons

1. Place all ingredients except sour cream and caviar in work bowl of food processor; process with steel blade until smooth (leaving a little texture from cabbage, if desired).
2. Pour into individual serving bowls; garnish each serving with a dollop of sour cream and ½ teaspoon whitefish or steelhead caviar. Serve well chilled.

Serves 4

Wild Greens Consommé

This recipe works very well with all kinds of freshly gathered tender young wild greens. Try them one at a time or in a motley combination. Accompany this soup with a very herbaceous sauvignon blanc or a first-rate pale ale.

Wild greens   6 ounces
Chicken stock (see Index)   6 to 8 cups
Nuoc mam   ½ teaspoon
Freshly ground black pepper   to taste
Nutmeg   ½ teaspoon
Lemon slices   garnish

1. Pull leaves of greens from stems. Discard tough stems but save tender ones. Wash and rinse leaves and tender stems well in cold water. Gather leaves and stems together and cut into thin strips (there should be 2 tightly packed cups of cut greens).
2. Heat stock. When liquid is at a simmer, add greens. Cook for 5 minutes, stirring regularly. Season with nuoc mam, pepper, and nutmeg. Serve in individual bowls. Float lemon slices on top.

Serves 4 to 6

Hop Shoot Soup

Hop shoots are usually pruned in the spring (only a few shoots are allowed to climb high on the trellises) and thrown out. But they are delicious and can be used like asparagus in many dishes. I particularly like this soup recipe. The soup should be accompanied by a well-chilled beer, of course.

Chicken stock (see Index)   8 cups
Hop shoots   2 cups coarsely chopped
Salt and freshly ground black pepper   to taste
Chervil or parsley   1 tablespoon chopped
Unsalted butter or sour cream (see Index)   garnish

1. Bring stock to boil in saucepan. Add all other ingredients except butter and return to boil. Simmer for about 5 minutes.
2. Serve hot with a dollop of butter or sour cream (hop shoots should still be crisp and somewhat crunchy).

Variations: Instead of hop shoots, use the tender, peeled young shoots of blackberry or salmonberry or the cleaned fiddleheads of bracken.

Serves 4 to 6

Chicken Broth with Sorrel and Poached Quail Eggs

The quality of this soup depends to some extent on an act of manual dexterity: the sorrel must be cut extremely fine, almost hair-fine, or it will be too heavy and will interfere with the eggs. Use a very sharp Chinese cleaver and roll the sorrel very tightly. Any somewhat sharp, dry cheese will go well with this broth. I like to use a tangy Briar Hills Cascadian goat cheese or a white (cow) Cheddar from Bandon or Rogue River. Accompany this soup with any dry white wine or with a good lager beer or a premium pale ale.

Chicken stock (see Index)   6 to 8 cups
Quail eggs   8 to 10
Sorrel   ¾ cup
Heavy cream   1 cup
Chives   1 tablespoon chopped
Chervil   2 tablespoons chopped
Nuoc mam   1 tablespoon
Freshly ground white pepper   to taste
Aged firm cheese   ¼ to ½ cup grated

1. Place stock in a saucepan and bring to a simmer. Poach quail eggs while stock is simmering (about 2 to 3 minutes). Place 1 or 2 quail eggs in each serving cup.
2. Bring stock to full boil. Add sorrel. Cook for 2 minutes. Turn off heat. Stir in cream. Gently spoon creamy broth over the eggs. Sprinkle each serving with chives, chervil, nuoc mam, and pepper. Top with grated cheese.

Serves 4 to 6

Green Pea and Sorrel Soup

The sorrel in this recipe adds a pleasant tang to the green peas, making it a much more complex dish than is to be expected from such rustic fare. Accompany the soup with home-baked french bread and a northwest sauvignon blanc, semillon, or a light pinot noir or lemberger. I like drinking a good lager beer or pale ale with this soup.

Unsalted butter (see Index)   1 tablespoon
Sorrel   1½ cups chopped and lightly packed
Nuoc mam   ½ teaspoon
Freshly ground black pepper   pinch
Leek   ½ cup finely chopped
Sweet onion   ½ cup chopped
Unsalted butter (see Index)   2 tablespoons
Split green peas   1½ cups
Lager beer or pale ale   2½ cups
Water   2½ cups
Nuoc mam   ½ teaspoon
Beef broth   1½ cups
Whipping cream   2 cups
Salt and freshly ground black pepper   to taste

1. In small saucepan, melt 1 tablespoon butter. Cook sorrel in butter until completely dry. Season with nuoc mam and pepper.
2. In a 3-quart dutch oven, cook leek and onion in 2 tablespoons butter until soft. Add peas, beer, water, and nuoc mam. Cover and cook in 375° oven until mixture is very soft, about 1½ hours. Stir occasionally.
3. Puree pea mixture in food processor; return to dutch oven. Stir in broth, cream, and sorrel. Heat through. Season to taste.

Serves 6

Split Pea Soup

There are few dishes that nourish and warm a tired hiker or boater more quickly than a good, thick split pea soup. This soup can be made with either green or yellow peas—either way it's one of my favorites. Accompany it with a premium lager beer.

Ham, bacon, or salt pork   1 cup cubed
Lovage   ½ cup coarsely chopped
Medium onion   1, chopped
Garlic clove   1, finely chopped
Split peas   2 cups
Thyme   ½ teaspoon or
    Dried thyme   ¼ teaspoon
Hot paprika   pinch
Bay leaf   1
Water   8 cups
Light soy sauce   1 teaspoon (or more)
Nuoc mam   ⅛ teaspoon
Freshly ground white pepper   to taste

1. In heavy cast-iron skillet, fry pork until crisp. Add lovage, onion, and garlic; fry until transparent. Do not brown.
2. Combine peas, thyme, paprika, bay leaf, and water in large kettle. Add pork/onion/lovage mixture. Season with soy sauce, nuoc mam, and pepper.
3. Boil vigorously for 20 minutes, then reduce heat, cover, and simmer until split peas are tender (watch the little blighters carefully—they stick and burn quite easily). Press soup through a fine sieve, reheat to boiling point (watch it!), and serve hot.

Serves 6 to 8

Lentil Soup

Ah, lentils, whose powerful fragrance seduced Esau into selling his birthright, whose rib-sticking goodness has succored many a weary traveler. I love lentils and I feel this soup is at its best when made with a good, hard-smoked beef sausage like the Hempler sausage available in northwest Washington or the Cape Ste. Ann sausage from Lopez Island; but it works equally well with other smoked, custom-made sausages (like Fred Bucheli's Matterhorn sausages in Yakima). Just make sure not to use a sausage that's too greasy or too watery—it'll ruin the taste of the dish. Serve this dish with a lusty red wine or a good ale or porter.

Lentils   2 cups, rinsed and picked over
Stale beer   2 cups
Water   3 cups
Chicken stock (see Index)   3 cups
Sausage   ½ pound, cubed
Sweet onion   ¾ cup chopped
Lovage   ½ cup chopped or
    Celery   ¾ cup chopped
Leeks   ½ cup chopped
Garlic glove   1, minced
Bay leaf   1
Thyme   1 teaspoon or
    Dried thyme   ½ teaspoon
Salt   to taste (if desired)
Freshly ground black pepper   ¼ teaspoon
Red wine vinegar   2 tablespoons or
    Aceto balsamico   3 tablespoons

1. Combine lentils with beer, water, and stock in large kettle. Bring to boil, reduce heat, and simmer 30 minutes, stirring occasionally.
2. Sauté sausage in heavy cast-iron skillet until somewhat crisp on outside. Add onion, lovage, leeks, garlic, bay leaf, and thyme. Cook and stir 4 minutes. Stir into lentils. (At this point a major division in the taste of lentil aficionados occurs: you either like your lentils whole or pulpy. If you like them whole, go on to step 3; if you like them pulpy, simmer soup for another 30 minutes, stirring quite regularly to make sure the darn things don't stick.)
3. Add salt, pepper, and vinegar. Return to simmer, then remove from heat.

Serves 8 to 12

Salads

Tossed Mixed Spring Salad

By early spring your body needs fresh, locally grown, vitamin-rich and mineral-filled greens to replenish itself. Wild as well as garden greens can supply the need. There's no fixed rule for making this salad: anything green and edible goes. The greens must be crisp and there should be just enough dressing to coat them.

Romaine lettuce   1 small head
Butter lettuce   1 small head
Radicchio   1 small head
Rocket (arugula) leaves   1 cup coarsely chopped
Spinach leaves   1 cup torn
Watercress leaves   1 cup coarsely chopped
Young thin asparagus or hop shoots   1 cup of 1-inch pieces parcooked
Light green violet leaves   ½ cup
Bracken fiddleheads   ½ to 1 cup cleaned and steamed
Sorrel or nasturtium leaves   ½ cup
Salmonberry shoots   ¼ cup chopped
Dandelion leaves   ½ cup
Olive oil   1 cup
White wine vinegar   ½ cup
Onion   1 tablespoon minced
Garlic cloves   1 to 4, finely minced (number depends on preference)
Freshly ground black pepper   ⅛ teaspoon
Nuoc mam   ½ teaspoon
Hot paprika   ¼ teaspoon
Herring roe   1 skein or
    Golden whitefish caviar   2 ounces

1. Tear romaine, butter lettuce, and radicchio into pieces; toss in large salad bowl with next 9 ingredients. Chill until ready to serve.
2. Mix all remaining ingredients except herring roe in a glass jar with tightly fitting lid. Strip herring roe of eggs; stir eggs into dressing. Shake dressing vigorously to blend well. Chill for several hours to let flavors develop. Shake again before tossing with greens. Add only enough dressing to coat greens.

Serves 6 to 8

Early Spring Dandelion Salad with Pacific Rock Scallop Roe

The Sooke Harbour House always experiments with interesting seafoods and wild greens. Here is a delectable spring salad from the restaurant's kitchen. This recipe calls only for the scallop's roe which is plentiful and very sweet in the early spring (use the scallops themselves for other dishes). Pick the dandelion leaves before flowers form (once dandelion flowers appear, the leaves become too bitter for salads).

Dandelion leaves   8 cups
Walnut or olive oil   4 tablespoons
Red wine vinegar   1 tablespoon
Meaux or Pommery mustard   1 tablespoon
Rock scallop roe*   from 4 large scallops
Garlic clove   ¼ teaspoon finely minced
Unsalted butter (see Index)   ½ tablespoon clarified

1. Wash and dry dandelion leaves. Make a vinaigrette by whisking together walnut oil, vinegar, and mustard. Pour over dandelion leaves and toss.
2. Cut roe into small chunks and sauté with garlic in heavy skillet over high heat in clarified butter for about 15 seconds.
3. Garnish salad with roe and serve immediately.

* The roe comes in 2 colors, red and orange. If you have a choice, use the deep red roe; it's more decorative.

Serves 4

Beer Potato Salad

It is very important to use a good lager beer (like Henry Weinhard's Private Reserve) for this dressing, or the flavor will be off. This salad is much improved if it is accompanied by tankards of the beer used in the dressing. Serve Beer Potato Salad as a side dish to barbecued meat or salmon.

Potatoes   3 pounds unskinned
Celery   1 cup diced
Japanese or English cucumber   1 cup diced
Small onion   1, chopped
Mayonnaise (see Index)   1 cup
Dijon, Meaux, or Pommery mustard   2 tablespoons
Hot pepper sauce   ¼ teaspoon
Lager beer   ½ cup
Chervil or parsley   1 teaspoon snipped or chopped
Chives   1 teaspoon thinly sliced
Mixed sprouts (adzuki, pea, mung, lentil)   1 cup

1. Cook potatoes until tender but still firm. When cool, peel and dice. Add celery, cucumber, and onion. Toss.
2. Blend together mayonnaise, mustard, and hot pepper sauce. Gradually stir in beer. Add chervil and chives. Blend well.
3. Gradually pour dressing over potato mixture. Toss lightly with 2 forks, being careful not to break potatoes. Chill for several hours to let flavors blend. When ready to serve, top with sprouts.

Serves 8 to 10

Rick O'Reilly's Potato Salad

This recipe, a favorite at La Petite Maison in Olympia, is enhanced by the shallots and mustard. Make sure to use a good Dijon mustard; turmeric-laden ballpark mustard will ruin the delicate flavor of the dish. If you eat this salad by itself, say, for a luncheon course, accompany it with a frothy glass of Ballard Bitter Ale.

Red new potatoes   2 pounds
Salt   to taste
Distilled white vinegar   2 tablespoons
Vegetable oil   6 tablespoons
Mustard   ¼ teaspoon
Shallots   3 tablespoons finely chopped
Salt and freshly ground black pepper   to taste
Parsley   garnish

1. Cover potatoes with water, salt to taste, and cook until done but still firm, about 20 minutes. Drain and set aside until ready to prepare.
2. Peel potatoes and cut into ¼-inch-thick slices.
3. Combine vinegar, oil, mustard, shallots, salt, and pepper in a mixing bowl and blend. Pour over potatoes.
4. Chill overnight. Stir from the bottom and garnish with parsley before serving.

Serves 4 to 6

Northwest Chef Salad

My wife, Victoria, enjoys a chef salad whenever she wants a light, but nourishing lunch. She has yet to find two chef salads that are alike. The quality of a chef salad depends on the quality, variety, and freshness of the ingredients; it is not merely a toss-up of greens and additives, but a dish that calls for a chef's best professional skills and imagination. Here's a recipe that combines the best features of several chef salads served at northwest restaurants.

Ripe cherry tomatoes   12
Salad greens (preferably from 2 or more different lettuces, including arugula, radicchio, endive, et al.)   8 cups torn
Green onions   ¼ cup sliced
Japanese cucumbers   2, thinly sliced
Mixed sprouts   ½ cup
Custom-made salami slices   4, cut into narrow strips
Farmhouse ham slices   4, cut into narrow strips
Pleasant Valley Gouda or other mild white cheese slices   4, cut into narrow strips
Northwest mozzarella or romano cheese slices   4, cut into narrow strips
Roast beef or pastrami slices   4, cut into narrow strips
Extrasharp white Cheddar cheese   ½ cup crumbled
Chicken, turkey, duck, or pheasant   ½ cup cooked
Northwest shrimp   1 cup cooked
Tiny clams   ½ cup steamed and shucked
Hazelnuts   ½ cup toasted and coarsely chopped
Water chestnuts*   ½ cup thinly sliced
Salmon caviar   4-ounce jar, drained
Salad dressing   as needed

1. Toss tomatoes (quarter them if they are on the large side), greens, green onions, cucumber, and sprouts together in a deep salad bowl. Divide into individual serving portions.
2. Top each with an equal share of the other ingredients, except dressing. Serve dressing on the side. Decorate each serving with a dollop of salmon caviar.

* Do not use canned water chestnuts.

Variations: Besides the ingredients listed in this recipe, you may want to add other delicacies such as pickled asparagus, hard-cooked egg, fresh peas and snow peas, sliced or cubed pickled beets, kelp pickles, sea snails, sea cucumber, toasted and crumbled nori, steamed pea crabs, and many others.

Serves 8 to 12

Helen's Kippered Salmon Salad

Here's a tasty recipe from La Petite Maison in Olympia, Washington. It goes very well with a chilled pinot noir blanc or Redhook Ale.

Smoked salmon   1 pound, broken into pieces
Bermuda onion   1, thinly sliced
Capers   2 tablespoons
Dill   2 teaspoons chopped
Mayonnaise (see Index)   ½ cup
Sour cream (see Index)   ½ cup
Freshly ground black pepper   to taste
Parsley   2 teaspoons chopped
Lemon slices   garnish
Lettuce leaves   garnish

1. Gently toss all ingredients, except for lemon slices and lettuce.
2. Chill and serve on lettuce leaves and garnish with lemon slices.

Serves 4

Flying Squid Salad

I enjoyed this salad at the Sooke Harbour House one New Year's Eve and I liked it so much, I asked for the recipe. Accompany this with a delicate dry white wine.

Squid*   one of about 3 pounds weight, frozen
Hazelnuts   ⅓ cup slivered
Celery   two 2-inch pieces, finely julienned
Radishes   12, sliced
Basil   1 teaspoon or
    Dried basil   ½ teaspoon
Rice vinegar   2 tablespoons
Olive oil   ¼ cup
Lemon juice   from ¼ lemon

1. Defrost squid in cold water. Place squid in large pan of boiling water, cover, and bring the water back to a gentle boil. Cook for approximately 15 minutes. When the tip of a sharp knife inserted into the meat has no resistance, the squid is ready. Drain and plunge into warm water to cool. Cut squid mantle into large pieces (first removing the thin outer membrane and the transparent quill). Slice into thin strips 2 inches long and refrigerate.
2. In a bowl, combine squid and remaining ingredients. Toss, arrange on small plates, and serve.

* Squid is one of my favorite seafoods, and the "flying" squid from Juan de Fuca Strait is among the best squid I have tasted. (Other tender squid may be substituted, of course.) The body meat from a 3-pound squid becomes quite tender after brief freezing.

Serves 4

Squid Salad

Accompany this salad with an off-dry Château Benoit or Worden's sauvignon blanc.

Squid mantle(s)*   1 pound, cleaned
Water   8 cups
Sauvignon blanc   1 tablespoon
Lovage   ½ cup finely cut
Green pepper or mild green chili   ½ cup cut into 1-inch-long slivers
Light soy sauce   1 tablespoon
Sesame oil   1 tablespoon
Cayenne   ¼ teaspoon

1. Slice mantle(s) open to flatten out. Remove quill. Thoroughly rinse mantle under cold running water. Place on a cutting board with inside (the less shiny) side facing up. With a very sharp knife, score hood diagonally at ¼-inch intervals. Turn mantle over and crosshatch the previous cuts, creating a diamond pattern. Do not cut all the way through and do not cut

straight downward, but cut at a 35-degree angle (this will raise the flesh in cooking and make an attractive "pine cone" pattern).

2. In a saucepan, bring 4 cups of water and the wine to a rolling boil. Drop in squid and blanch for 30 seconds. Remove, rinse thoroughly with cold water, and drain on paper towels.
3. Cut mantle lengthwise into halves; then cut each half crosswise into ½-inch strips. Repeat until all squid has been cut into strips.
4. Bring another 4 cups of water to a boil and blanch the lovage and green pepper for 15 seconds. Remove with skimmer, rinse with cold water, and drain.
5. In a small mixing bowl, combine soy sauce, sesame oil, and cayenne. Stir to blend well. Toss squid, lovage, and green pepper in mixture; serve at room temperature.

* This dish works as well with the small squid found in Puget Sound and along the outer coast, as with the large, tender "flying" squid of Juan de Fuca Strait. If small squid are used, cut off tentacles ¾-inch from head and again just below eyes. This will leave a ring of meat to which tentacle stubs are attached. Remove beak (lodged inside ring) by pressing out with fingers. Heat butter in heavy cast-iron skillet. Place squid rings in pan, tentacles up. Sauté briefly; the tentacles should bend down, making the rings look like open "flowers." Use to garnish the salad.

Serves 4

Chilled Crab Salad

It seems that just about everyone who crabs a lot ends up with a surplus of fresh crab. If you don't like to freeze crab—I don't—try this way of finishing up your leftover crab. Enjoy it with a well-chilled premium beer.

Large Dungeness crabs   2, cooked, disjointed, and cracked (save "butter" inside shell)
Olive oil   1 cup
White wine vinegar   ¾ cup
Garlic cloves   2, finely minced
Chervil or parsley   ¼ cup chopped
Chives   ¼ cup thinly sliced
Lemon   1, thinly sliced
Oregano   1 teaspoon
Freshly ground black pepper   1 teaspoon
Nuoc mam   ¼ teaspoon

1. Place crab in shallow bowl and add other ingredients. Toss.
2. Cover and refrigerate at least 1 hour. Serve.

Serves 6 to 8

Crab Meat and Cucumber Salad

This simple salad can be served with two different dressings: a simple vinegar, soy sauce, and lemon dressing (see dressing for Summer Fruit and Seafood Salad) or a more adventuresome Sea Urchin Dressing. Use the light dressing when serving the salad before a light luncheon dish; serve it with the Sea Urchin Dressing when it precedes a more complex dinner entrée.

Japanese cucumber   1
Fresh Dungeness or rock crab meat   6 ounces
Sea Urchin Dressing

1. Cut cucumbers into very fine slices and soak in salted water (2 tablespoons salt to 1 quart water) for 15 minutes. Squeeze to drain. Cucumber slices should be limp.
2. Pick over crab meat to remove all cartilage; pull meat apart into fine shreds.
3. Combine crab meat and cucumber. Divide into 4 equal portions and place in individual serving bowls. Spoon on dressing. (Two tablespoons vinegar dressing or 4 teaspoons Sea Urchin Dressing.) Toss. Serve chilled.

Serves 4

Sea Urchin Dressing

Sea urchin roe   ⅓ cup
Egg yolk   1, lightly beaten
Mirin   2 teaspoons
Sake   2 teaspoons

Rub sea urchin roe through fine sieve with back of a spoon. Blend egg yolk into roe puree. Blend in mirin and sake, beating with fork until smooth. Must be used immediately.

Makes ½ cup

Summer Fruit and Seafood Salad

This is a whopper of a salad—it can easily serve as the main course at a luncheon. On a warm or hot day, it will refresh the palate and nourish without overloading the system. The pleasant acidity of a Japanese sunomono dressing and the tartness of just-ripe fruit go very well with the delicate taste of fresh raw seafood. You may, of course, steam or parboil the seafood if you have an aversion to raw fish and shellfish. Flavors and textures will not be as sophisticated, but the dish will still be delicious. Accompany this salad with a first-rate sake, lager beer, or light ale.

Japanese cucumber   1
Belly meat of 1 large geoduck   cleaned and sliced into ¹⁄₁₆-inch-thick slices
Feet of steamed or barbecued limpets, ½ to 1 inch in length   12, lightly pounded and cut
into thin strips
Feet of cockles   12, cleaned, lightly pounded, and quartered
Rings cut from the mantles of tiny squid   12, cleaned and parboiled for 15 seconds
Raw, tiny deveined shrimp or raw prawns   ½ cup cubed
Raw tuna *(maguro)*   ½ cup cut into thin strips
Cooked Dungeness or rock crab   ½ cup cubed
Small subripe nectarine or peach   1, peeled, quartered, and cut into ⅛-inch-thick slices
Small subripe apricots   2, peeled, cut into ⅛-inch-thick slices
Just ripe plums   2, cut into ⅛-inch slices
Firm, just ripe strawberries   12, destemmed and cut into ¼-inch-thick slices
Dressing
Salmon caviar   6 to 8 teaspoons drained

1. Finely slice cucumber and soak in salted water (2 tablespoons salt in 1 quart water) for 15
   minutes. Squeeze to drain. Cucumber slices should be limp.
2. Combine cucumber, seafood, and fruit. Toss. Divide into 6 to 8 serving bowls.
3. Sprinkle Dressing over individual servings. Be careful with the amount you use. Start with a
   little and add more to taste. (Too little and the taste is incomplete; too much and the taste of
   the seafood and fruit is lost. Let your taste buds be your guide—there are no fixed rules.)
4. Top each portion with a teaspoon of salmon caviar.

Serves 6 to 8

Dressing

Hon-mirin   1½ tablespoons
Rice vinegar   ½ cup
Light soy sauce   2 tablespoons
Lemon juice   1½ tablespoons
Cold water   ½ to ⅔ cup

Mix mirin, rice vinegar, and soy sauce in saucepan. Heat just to a boil, stir, remove from heat
and cool to room temperature. Stir in lemon juice. Thin with water to desired level of acidity.

Makes 1½ cups

Marinated Mushroom Salad

This salad is best when made with a variety of wild mushrooms, but commercially available white mushrooms, shiitake, oyster mushrooms, or enokitake may also be used.

Large meadow mushrooms   ¼ pound
Blewit mushrooms   ¼ pound
Chanterelle mushrooms   ¼ pound
Matsutake or shiitake mushrooms   ¼ pound
Lemon juice   from ½ lemon
Parsley   2 tablespoons snipped or chopped
Chives   2 tablespoons finely cut or
    Chinese chives   1½ tablespoons finely cut
Vinaigrette Dressing
Ripe tomatoes   2, sliced or
    Ripe cherry tomatoes   8, halved

Slice mushrooms and toss with lemon juice. Add parsley, chives, and Vinaigrette Dressing. Toss, chill for 1 or 2 hours, then toss again before serving. Garnish with a few tomato slices.

Serves 4

Vinaigrette Dressing

White wine vinegar   3 tablespoons
Dijon-style mustard   1 teaspoon
Olive oil   1 cup
Sauvignon blanc   dash
Salt and freshly ground white pepper   to taste

Blend together vinegar and mustard. Gradually add oil, pouring in a thin stream and beating with whisk until mixture thickens slightly. Beat in wine and season to taste with salt and pepper.

Makes about 1⅓ cups

Garlic Dressing

I really like garlic—the more the better—and I'm also really glad that garlic is good for the system, because I'd eat it even if it weren't. But not to worry. The ancient Egyptians fed large quantities of the noble bulbs to the workers who built the pyramids; Aristophanes wrote that athletes ate garlic before exercising in the stadium; Virgil recommended it for maintaining the strength of harvest workers; Pliny maintained garlic as a cure for consumption, Celsius as a cure for fever; Hippocrates called it a perspirant and Dioscorides favored it as a wormer. The prophet Mohammed thought it helped against stings and bites by poisonous animals, and Culpeper concurred. The upshot of all this talk is that you should eat lots of garlic, as often as possible, especially since garlic grows very well in the Pacific Northwest.

Olive oil   1 cup
White wine vinegar   ¼ cup
Dijon or Pommery mustard   1 teaspoon
Garlic cloves   4 to 12 (or more), crushed in a garlic press
Nuoc mam   1 teaspoon
Freshly ground white pepper   to taste

Combine all ingredients in a tightly closed jar. Shake vigorously until blended. Let rest for an hour or so to let flavors develop, then shake again and serve.

Makes about 1¼ cups

Elephant Garlic Dressing

Elephant garlic, a larger and milder version of our regular kitchen garlic (with a somewhat different pungency), grows very well in the Pacific Northwest. I like to use it in tangy salad dressings like this one—a perfect complement to garden or wild greens. A dry northwest sauvignon blanc or semillon will hold up quite well to a garlicky dressing, but so will a good beer or ale.

Mayonnaise (see Index)   1 cup
Dijon-style mustard   ½ teaspoon
Lemon juice   1 tablespoon
Red wine vinegar   1 tablespoon
Freshly ground black pepper   1 teaspoon
Elephant garlic cloves   4 to 6, crushed in a garlic press
Egg yolk (preferably from a fresh duck egg)   1
Salt or nuoc mam   to taste

Combine mayonnaise, mustard, lemon juice, vinegar, pepper, garlic, and egg yolk. Whip well with wire whisk. Season to taste with salt or nuoc mam. Whip again to blend. Chill thoroughly before serving.

Makes about 1½ cups

Dill Dressing

Dill is a popular herb in the cookery of the Pacific Northwest's Scandinavian population. This dressing goes well with chilled fish, crustaceans, or shellfish.

Mayonnaise (see Index)   2 cups
Dill   ¼ cup chopped
White wine vinegar   ¼ cup
Dijon or Düsseldorf mustard   2½ teaspoons

Place mayonnaise in bowl and stir in dill, vinegar, and mustard. Beat until fluffy. Chill well before serving.

Makes about 2¼ cups

Cranberry Vinaigrette

This salad dressing is served regularly with impeccably fresh greens at the Shelburne Inn Restaurant. It adds a lovely, fruity touch.

Cranberries   2 cups
Water   ½ cup
Sugar   2 tablespoons
Oil   2 cups
Red wine vinegar   ½ cup
Raspberry wine vinegar   ⅓ cup
Salt and freshly ground white pepper   to taste

Boil together cranberries, water, and sugar until cranberries split open; strain excess liquid. Puree cranberries. Stir in oil and vinegars. Season to taste with salt and white pepper.

Makes 5½ cups

Oregon Blue Cheese Dressing

You may want to use a very ripe Oregon blue cheese for this dressing (you'll have to ripen it yourself, since it usually comes from the cheese factory before it is old) so that the rich smoky taste can dominate the dressing.

Vegetable oil   1 cup
Wine vinegar   ¼ cup
Cold water   3 tablespoons
Dijon-style mustard   ½ teaspoon
Freshly ground black pepper   to taste
Salt   to taste
Worcestershire sauce   1¼ teaspoons (optional)
Hot chili sauce   1 teaspoon
Onion   1 teaspoon grated
Oregon blue cheese   2 ounces, crumbled

1. Combine oil, vinegar, and water and beat (or shake in closed jar) until blended.
2. Add all other ingredients except onion and cheese and beat until blended.
3. Add onion and beat well.
4. Add blue cheese and beat until creamy and smooth.

Makes about 1½ cups

Yogurt Dressing

This is a low-calorie—though seemingly rich—dressing. It can do double-duty as a dip for crisp raw vegetables, freshly cooked shrimp, and for such tart fruits as sliced green apples.

Plain yogurt   8-ounce carton
Onion   ⅓ cup finely chopped
Small clove garlic   1, minced
Lovage leaves   ¼ cup finely cut
Chervil or parsley   ¼ cup finely snipped or chopped
Salt   to taste

Blend all ingredients. Chill to blend flavors (about 2 or more hours). Stir well just before serving.

Makes 1½ cups

Egg Dishes

Buttermilk Scrambled Eggs

This is my wife's favorite scrambled egg recipe. It makes for exceptionally fluffy eggs.

Duck or chicken eggs   3
Unsalted butter (see Index)   1 tablespoon
Cultured buttermilk   2 tablespoons
Tabasco sauce   dash
Freshly ground black pepper   ¼ teaspoon
Dried fines herbes   ¼ teaspoon

1. Lightly beat eggs together; melt butter over low heat and add eggs.
2. After eggs have become slightly firm, add buttermilk, and stir well to distribute it evenly in the egg mixture.
3. Add Tabasco, pepper, and fines herbes.
4. Stir mixture occasionally to avoid sticking, until eggs reach desired doneness.

Serves 1 to 2

Two Caviar Scrambled Eggs and Peas

This dish is very good with duck eggs, but chicken eggs may be used instead, though the flavor of the dish will be milder. Accompany this dish with a spicy, dry gewürztraminer.

Green peas   1 cup
Vegetable oil   as needed
Smoked country ham slice   1, diced
Country bacon slice   1, diced
Chives   1 tablespoon chopped
Freshly ground white pepper   ¼ teaspoon
Duck eggs   6, lightly beaten
Whitefish caviar   3 teaspoons drained
Dry gewürztraminer   1 tablespoon
Salmon caviar or other fish roe   3 teaspoons drained

1. Boil peas until tender. Set aside.
2. Heat a little oil in a heavy cast-iron pot or in a Chinese sandy pot; gently fry ham, bacon, and peas; sprinkle with chives and pepper. Fry for a few seconds longer. Stir in eggs and whitefish caviar. Add wine, stirring constantly.
3. When eggs begin to set, but are still moist, move from pan to serving dish. (They will continue to cook from their own heat, reaching the right consistency by the time they are served.)
4. Top each serving with ½ to 1 teaspoon of salmon caviar. Sprinkle with more chives, if desired.

Serves 4 to 6

Sucker Roe and Scrambled Eggs

Both the roe and milt of suckers are delicious, but you'll have to procure this tasty treat yourself ("First catch yourself a sucker . . .") unless you run across it in a Chinese fish market.

Sucker roe*   2, cleaned
Unsalted butter (see Index)   2 tablespoons
Eggs   2
Chives   ½ teaspoon chopped
Salt and freshly ground black pepper   to taste

1. Fry roe in butter until almost opaque.
2. Break eggs into bowl and mix with fork. Add eggs to roe; scramble both.
3. Sprinkle chives over eggs and mix them in as you toss eggs in pan.
4. Season with salt and pepper to taste. Serve with buttered toast.

* Make sure the roe are intact, clean, and uniform in color. Carefully remove the membrane enclosing the eggs and any connective tissue and veins. Rinse eggs gently in cold water. Drain on paper toweling. The eggs should stick together on their own and be firm. If they are fully ripe and ready to separate from the membrane, their texture and flavor will not be as fine. Roe exceeding 1 inch in thickness should be parboiled for 5 to 6 minutes before membrane is removed (prick with fork like a sausage).

Serves 2

Rich Duck Egg Foo Yung

The duck eggs add an extra richness to this dish, but extra-large chicken eggs may be used as a substitute. Cover these sumptuous omelets with a cream sauce and accompany them with hot cinnamon rolls and a good Chinese tea.

Mung bean sprouts   2 cups
Vegetable oil or butter   as needed
Gingerroot   1 slice, minced
Scallions   6, chopped
Celery stalk   1, sliced paper thin on the bias
Shiitake or chanterelle mushrooms   2, sliced
Salt and freshly ground black pepper   to taste
Smoked country ham   ½ cup finely diced
Dungeness crab meat   1 cup shredded
Duck eggs   8
Apple Cream Sauce

1. Break bean sprouts in half (if you feel energetic, remove the long thin root at tip of sprout). Heat a little oil in heavy skillet and fry all ingredients except eggs and sauce for 3 to 5 minutes (or until scallions are cooked). Remove from heat.
2. Beat eggs well and stir in cooked ingredients.
3. Heat more oil in skillet, pour in enough egg mixture to form a small "frittata," and fry on both sides until golden brown. Repeat until all egg mixture is cooked.
4. Cover with Apple Cream Sauce and serve.

Serves 4 to 6

Apple Cream Sauce

Unsalted butter (see Index)   ¼ cup
Sauvignon blanc   ¼ cup
Shiitake mushrooms   1 cup sliced
Large green cooking apple   1, cored, peeled, and diced
Heavy cream   1 cup
Salt and freshly ground black pepper   to taste

Melt butter in heavy skillet, add wine, mushrooms, and apple. Cook over high heat until most of liquid evaporates (do not burn or brown; lift pan from heat if butter becomes too hot). Turn heat to low. Add cream, stir, and heat gently (do not boil, or cream may curdle). Season with salt and pepper to taste.

Makes 3 to 3½ cups

Ancient ("Thousand-Year-Old") Eggs

Different types of preserved eggs are sold in oriental food markets throughout the Pacific Northwest. They are becoming increasingly popular in baked goods and as appetizers (with soy sauce, vinegar, and chopped gingerroot on the side), partly because they are so much more affordable here than they are in Asia. But if you live in a place where these peculiar delicacies are still unknown or unavailable on a regular basis, here's an easy (though time-consuming) recipe for making your own. Oh, by the way, it is said that this recipe works best and that the eggs are tastiest if you live like a hermit, shunning strangers and talking as little as possible, while these eggs "ripen."

Coarse tea leaves   as needed to make 1 part
Pinewood ashes   1 part
Hardwood charcoal ashes   1 part
Kitchen stove ashes   1 part
Lime   ½ part
Duck eggs   as needed
Salt   ½ teaspoon per egg

1. Brew a strong tea from tea leaves; strain; mix with equal parts ashes and ½ part lime. Add correct proportion of salt for number of eggs, plus 1 teaspoon extra for every 6 eggs. Coat each egg with a thick layer of this mudlike mixture.
2. Line large earthenware container (available in Chinatowns) with clean loam. Carefully place eggs on a layer of loam (allow 2 inches between each egg). Fill space between eggs with loam; place 4-inch layer of loam atop eggs. Continue until jar is full. Keep container in cool dark place for 100 days—eggs should then be ready.

Blue Cheese Yogurt Soufflé

The rich, smoky undertaste of a very ripe Oregon blue cheese really enhances the flavor of this dish. If you cannot obtain the proper firm cheese—a well-aged Bandon or Rogue River white Cheddar—use a good Gruyère cheese instead. Accompany this soufflé with a mature northwest cabernet sauvignon or merlot.

Sharp white Cheddar cheese   ⅓ cup grated
Unsalted butter (see Index)   ⅓ cup
Pastry flour   ½ cup
Whole milk   ¾ cup
Plain low-fat yogurt   1 cup
Oregon blue cheese   1 cup crumbled
Hot paprika   pinch
Medium egg yolks   4
Medium egg whites   5

1. Lightly grease a 7- or 8-inch soufflé dish. Sprinkle bottom of dish with Cheddar.
2. Tear off a sheet of cooking parchment 2 inches longer than the circumference of the dish. Fold lengthwise into thirds. Lightly grease one side. Wrap parchment around outside of soufflé dish, greased side facing inward, letting a 2-inch rim extend above top edge. Secure with butcher twine.
3. Melt butter in small saucepan and stir in flour. Slowly add milk and half the yogurt, stirring constantly until thickened. Stir in blue cheese, remaining yogurt, and hot paprika.
4. Beat egg yolks lightly. Pour a small amount of yogurt mixture into yolks. Stir well and return to rest of yogurt mixture. Cook 1 minute, stirring constantly. Beat egg whites until they form soft peaks. Fold into yolk mixture. Do not overmix.
5. Pour mixture into soufflé dish. Bake at 350° for 40 to 50 minutes, or until done. Serve immediately.

Serves 6

Steamed Egg Custard

This is a favorite recipe of the Chinese community, but it deserves to be known more widely.

Scallions 4 stalks
Duck eggs 4
Salt and freshly ground black pepper   to taste
Chicken stock (see Index) 2 cups hot
Light soy sauce 2 teaspoons
Lemon juice 2 teaspoons

1. Chop scallions, including most of the green part (cut off dry or discolored or mushy tips).
2. Beat eggs, season with salt and pepper, then slowly pour in hot stock, stirring constantly. Pour into attractive greased serving dish, sprinkle with scallions, and steam on rack in wok or in bamboo steamer 15 to 20 minutes. Sprinkle with either soy sauce, lemon juice, or a combination and serve.

Note: When making steamed custards, always use hot liquids with the eggs. This will give a creamy texture; cold liquids cause air holes and a lumpy texture.

Serves 2 to 4

Coin Purse Eggs

These eggs derive their name from their close resemblance to a Chinese coin purse. The egg white represents the purse and the egg yolk within represents the golden coin. We've changed this classic dish somewhat by spilling some of the "gold" out of the purse.

Vegetable oil   as needed
Duck eggs   8 to 12 (2 per serving)
Freshly ground black pepper   to taste
Light soy sauce   as needed
Chervil or parsley   ½ to ¾ cup chopped
Salmon caviar   8 to 12 teaspoons drained
Lemon wedges   4 to 6

1. Heat a little oil in wok. Carefully break 1 egg in center of pan. Sprinkle with pepper. When egg white has firmed below, but upper surface is still moist, flip half of egg over the other to form a semicircle. Fry egg on both sides until golden. Set aside. Repeat with remaining eggs. Keep heat low during initial cooking and raise it when egg has been folded (this will help color the eggs).
2. Sprinkle eggs with a little soy sauce and chervil; spoon on a teaspoon of salmon caviar. Serve with 1 lemon wedge for each 2 eggs.

Serves 4 to 6

Vegetable
Dishes

Nettles in Butter and Cream

This is an early spring dish, to be eaten when nettle leaves are young and tender (before the plants flower). Be sure to wear gloves and be very careful when collecting nettles; you don't want your hands burnt (if you burn yourself, chew up some fresh dock and apply it to the burn—it works for me).

Tender nettle leaves*   2 pounds
Unsalted butter (see Index)   ⅓ cup, melted
Nuoc mam   1 to 2 teaspoons
Nutmeg   sprinkle
Freshly ground black pepper   to taste (optional)
Whipping cream   1½ cups
Timbale Cases   8, prebaked
Sour cream (see Index)   3 tablespoons
Salmon or steelhead caviar   4 teaspoons drained

1. Parboil nettles in plenty of water; drain and let cool. Press all water from nettle leaves; chop leaves finely.
2. In saucepan, combine nettles with melted butter. Cook over medium heat until leaves dry. Do not burn. Season with nuoc mam and nutmeg (and pepper to taste, if desired). Turn heat to low; add cream and cook for 10 minutes.
3. Spoon into timbales and top each with a teaspoon of sour cream and ½ teaspoon salmon or steelhead caviar.

* Fortunately, cooking takes the sting out of nettles. Discard the tough and fibrous stems—they make better dental floss than food. (If you cannot find a sufficient quantity of nettles or are leery of gathering the herb, use other tender wild greens or, as a last resort, fresh spinach.)

Serves 8

Timbale Cases

Timbale dishes can be served straight in a metal or porcelain dish, or they may be unmolded like custard. But according to Larousse Gastronimique *"the true gourmand is not satisfied with a* timbale *whose crust is not edible; when served with a real* timbale, *he enjoys not only the contents but the container, too." Timbales may be filled before cooking with forcemeats, or they may be filled after the shells have been baked. Any unsweetened pie dough will do, but here's my favorite.*

Flour   2¼ cups
Salt   pinch
Unsalted butter (see Index)   ½ cup plus 1 tablespoon, cut into small pieces
Small egg   1
Ice water   3 to 5 tablespoons

1. Sift flour and salt into large bowl. With pastry blender (or 2 knives), cut butter into flour/salt mixture until evenly distributed and mixture resembles bread crumbs. With a fork, lightly mix in egg and just enough ice water to bind dough. Press into a ball and wrap in foil or plastic wrap. Refrigerate 2 hours.
2. Preheat oven to 400°. On a floured surface, roll out dough about ⅛-inch thick. Cut out 16 circles, 4 inches across. Place in 16 small soufflé dishes, fluted tartlet pans, or muffin pan cups. Press down edges well. Prick with fork all over. Bake 15 to 20 minutes, or until shells are golden brown. (Prick shells well to make sure they do not form bubbles.)

Makes 16

Zucchini Stuffed with Seasoned Cream Cheese

I developed this recipe one day when I had made up a batch of fresh herbed cream cheese and was given a number of small zucchini by a friend. It is important to cook the zucchini only long enough to tenderize them a bit, but not so long that they lose their crunch and become soggy.

Small (5- to 7-inch) zucchini   3
Seasoned Cream Cheese (see Index)   ½ cup (more or less)
Sweet sherry   3 teaspoons
Nuoc mam   ½ teaspoon
Freshly ground black pepper   to taste

1. Halve zucchini lengthwise. Scoop out pulp, leaving 6 shells with about ¼-inch-thick walls.
2. Chop half the pulp; combine with cream cheese, sherry, nuoc mam, and pepper. Fill zucchini shells with cream cheese mixture, forming a low mound.
3. Serve raw or bake in 350° oven for 20 minutes (cheese should be melted and zucchini should still be crunchy).

Serves 6 as a side dish

Zucchini Stuffed with Fresh Sweet Corn

This is a great dish to eat after a day of picking fresh sweet corn in the Yakima Valley. It's perfect for a warm summer evening and calls for crisp chips and lots of cold beer to accompany it.

Zucchini (preferably short fat ones)   six, 4 ounces each
Sweet corn   2 cups, cooked and freshly shucked
Medium eggs   2
Thick cream or crème fraîche (see Index)   2 tablespoons
Salt   to taste
Cream cheese (see Index)   4 ounces, softened
White Jack cheese or queso blanco   2 ounces, grated or crumbled
Unsalted butter (see Index)   3 tablespoons, softened
Yakima Valley Hot Tomato Sauce

1. Preheat oven to 350°.
2. Clean and trim zucchini. Halve lengthwise and scoop out inner flesh, leaving a shell about ½-inch thick. Discard pulp.
3. Place zucchini in a shallow oven-proof dish just large enough to hold shells in 1 layer. Set aside while you prepare filling.
4. Blend corn, eggs, cream, and salt into coarse puree in food processor. Combine with cream cheese.
5. Fill zucchini shells with corn stuffing. Sprinkle with cheese and dot with butter.
6. Cover dish with foil and set into oven. Bake until squash is tender, but still slightly crunchy, about 30 minutes. Serve covered with tomato sauce.

Serves 8 to 12

Yakima Valley Hot Tomato Sauce

Vine-ripened tomatoes*   three, about 1 pound total, broiled
Medium onion   ¼, roughly chopped
Small garlic clove   1, roughly chopped
Chili poblanos**   2, roasted, peeled, and roughly chopped
Salt   to taste
Comino   ¼ teaspoon crushed
Coriander leaves   1 teaspoon finely chopped (optional)
Vegetable oil   2 tablespoons

1. Blend all ingredients except oil until fairly smooth (best done by hand, so sauce retains some texture).
2. Heat oil in heavy skillet, add sauce, and cook over medium flame for about 8 minutes, until sauce has thickened and is well seasoned.

* To broil tomatoes, place whole tomatoes under broiler until skin is wrinkled and brown and flesh is soft right through (about 20 to 25 minutes for an 8-ounce tomato). This is best done on a griddle over an aromatic wood fire, or it can be done in a metal pan over hot coals in a barbecue. A kitchen oven will also work, though the flavor is not as fine. Turn tomatoes occasionally to blister evenly. Do not peel (you may, however, remove the worst black spots and scorched areas). Grind in mortar or bowl.

** To roast and skin peppers, place on griddle or grill over high heat (I use a small roasting grill). Turn often to scorch evenly. When skin is black and scorched, it will come off easily. Destem pepper and remove seeds unless you want sauce to be very hot. Remember, you must be sure to wash your hands thoroughly after handling hot peppers to prevent rubbing pepper juice into eyes or sensitive skin areas.

Makes 2 cups

Chopped Yakima Valley Zucchini and Tomatoes

This is a recipe that should be made with the fresh produce of the land when it is at its best, with vine-ripened tomatoes and peppers and with small tender zucchini. It is a dish that can be as hot as you want it to be: the serrano peppers are cooked whole with the vegetables, imparting a delicate, flavorful spiciness. If you want the dish to be very hot, chop the peppers after cooking and add them to the dish.

Vegetable oil   3 to 4 teaspoons
Vine-ripened tomatoes*   1½ pounds
Garlic clove   1, finely chopped
Zucchini   1½ pounds cleaned, trimmed, and cut into ½-inch cubes
Medium yellow onion   1, finely chopped
Whole serrano chilies   2
Salt   to taste

1. Heat oil until it just begins to smoke. Remove from heat and let it cool a little while you prepare vegetables.
2. Peel and seed tomatoes. Strain juice from seeds into bowl. Save.
3. Return pan to burner. Add chopped tomatoes, juice, garlic, zucchini, onion, chilies, and salt.
4. Cover pan and cook vegetables over medium heat for 5 minutes; then uncover and cook until zucchini is tender but still slightly crunchy, about another 3 minutes maximum.
5. Scrape bottom of pan and stir mixture well from time to time so that it does not stick.

* Cherry tomatoes may be substituted for the chopped tomato. Make sure these do not burst in cooking.

Serves 6 to 8

Zucchini and Cherry Tomatoes with Garlic and Matsutake

*Cherry tomatoes, zucchini, and herbs are among the few plants that do well on my apartment deck—which means that we eat a lot of them. Here's an interesting variation I came up with when the Mushroom Man, Steve Czarnecki, brought me some early matsutake (*Armillaria ponderosa*). This recipe also works quite well with other mushrooms (such as the horse mushroom,* Agaricus arvensis*).*

Firm, unblemished small zucchini   two, about ¾ pound
Olive oil   3 tablespoons
Salt and freshly ground black pepper   to taste
Garlic cloves   2, peeled (or more—I usually like 12)
Cherry tomatoes   16
Medium matsutake mushrooms   2, very coarsely chopped (½- to ¾-inch pieces)

1. Trim ends from zucchini. Quarter zucchini lengthwise. Cut each quarter into ½-inch lengths. There should be about 3½ cups.
2. Heat oil in a large skillet.
3. Add zucchini pieces to hot oil. Sprinkle with salt and pepper to taste.
4. Add garlic and cook, shaking skillet and stirring until zucchini starts to brown, about 5 minutes.
5. Add tomatoes and matsutake and continue to cook, stirring gently so tomatoes cook evenly without breaking skin. Cook about 2 minutes, just until tomatoes are heated. Do not overcook or tomatoes will break and mushrooms will become soggy.
6. Remove and discard garlic and serve.

Serves 4

Drunken Zucchini

Good beer is probably one of our least appreciated cooking ingredients. In the following recipe, it adds a pleasantly bitter hop taste to the zucchini (if you are not fond of delicate bitterness in your food, use a dry wine instead). I used Henry Weinhard's Private Reserve, but any good lager beer will do.

Unsalted butter (see Index)   ½ tablespoon
Olive oil   ½ tablespoon
Small zucchini   3, coarsely diced
Lager beer   ¼ cup
Nuoc mam   1 teaspoon
Freshly ground Tellicherry pepper   to taste

1. Heat butter and oil over high heat until very hot. Add zucchini; cook, turning constantly, for 1 minute. Add beer. Then add nuoc mam and pepper.
2. Cook, tossing constantly, until pan juices are just about gone and zucchini is slightly browned. Serve hot.

Serves 4 to 6

Eggplant and Clams

This recipe combines foods from both sides of the mountains: clams from the saltwater beaches and eggplant from the hot interior valleys. It is very good accompanied by a dry or slightly off-dry northwest sauvignon blanc or semillon.

Large eggplants   2
Geoduck, horse clams, or butter clams   2 cups minced
Cracker crumbs   2 cups
Unsalted butter (see Index)   2 tablespoons, melted
Medium eggs   2, beaten
Salt and freshly ground black pepper   to taste
Cream or half-and-half   2 tablespoons (optional)
Unsalted butter (see Index)   2 tablespoons

1. Peel eggplant; cut into 1-inch-thick slices. Cover with water for 20 minutes.
2. Remove from water. Steam (or boil) for about 15 minutes or until soft, drain, and mash. Add clams, 1½ cups of cracker crumbs, 2 tablespoons melted butter, eggs, salt, and pepper; moisten with cream if mixture seems dry.
3. Place in 2-quart baking pan or in individual ramekins. Cover with remaining crumbs. Dot with 2 tablespoons butter and bake in 325° oven until brown, about 30 to 45 minutes.

Serves 6

Bob Meade's Rosemary Potatoes

Bob Meade, well-known proprietor of Le Cuisinier Cooking School in Bellingham, brought this dish to a lamb and kid barbecue in Bellingham last year. It was perfect for accompanying both. Serve it with a full-bodied Kiona lemberger.

Baking potatoes   2 pounds
Large yellow onions (not Walla Walla Sweets)   2
Extra virgin olive oil (preferably Provençal)   ⅓ cup
Dried rosemary   2 teaspoons finely ground
Salt and freshly ground black pepper   to taste

1. Cut potatoes into thick (¼- to ½-inch) slices. Simmer in water until they begin to get tender (about 10 to 12 minutes). Drain and keep warm.
2. Coarsely chop onions; sauté in olive oil until golden. Stir in rosemary and cook for a couple of minutes more.
3. Carefully mix onions and potatoes, making sure potatoes do not break. Place mixture in a baking dish (potatoes should lie as flat as possible); season with salt and pepper to taste.
4. Bake at 350° until tender (about 30 minutes).

Serves 4 to 6

Lemon Potatoes

This recipe calls for new potatoes and for an herb that grows particularly well in coastal areas of the Pacific Northwest, lemon thyme. Use only freshly squeezed lemon juice and garden-fresh herbs.

New potatoes   1½ pounds, unpeeled and cut into quarters
Garlic cloves   4, finely chopped
Lemon juice   2 tablespoons
Green onions   ¼ cup sliced
Unsalted butter (see Index)   2 tablespoons
Lemon thyme   2 tablespoons chopped
Dill   1 teaspoon chopped
Nuoc mam   ½ teaspoon

1. In large skillet, cover potatoes and garlic with water and cook until done (but not overcooked). Drain. Sprinkle with 1 tablespoon lemon juice; toss well to cover.
2. In same skillet, sauté green onion in butter with lemon thyme, dill, and nuoc mam. Add potatoes, garlic, and remaining lemon juice. Toss and heat.

Serves 4

Potato Cheese Bake

Cheese and potatoes seem to have an affinity for each other which—though firmly established in such classic dishes as puree de pommes de terre au gratin, pommes de terre au fromage, gratinees, and gratin dauphinois—sometimes escapes the general eating public. Several of our superb northwest cheeses go very well with potatoes—say a white Cheddar from Bandon or the Rogue River Creamery, or the excellent goat cheeses made by Briar Hills Dairy in Chehalis. All will work well in the following recipe.

Unsalted butter (see Index)   ¼ cup
Freshly ground white pepper   ¼ teaspoon
Baking potatoes   3 cups cut into ⅛-inch slices
Light soy sauce   ½ teaspoon
Cheese   2 tablespoons grated or crumbled
Red bell pepper*   2 tablespoons diced
Chervil or parsley   2 tablespoons finely chopped

1. Preheat oven to 350°.
2. Melt butter in 12- by 8-inch baking dish (use either a flame-proof dish on top of stove or melt in oven, about 5 to 7 minutes). Remove from heat as soon as butter has melted (do not brown). Stir in pepper. Add potatoes and toss until coated with butter. Cover with foil; bake for 40 minutes.
3. Remove foil; add soy sauce and toss again; sprinkle with cheese. Continue baking, uncovered, for 10 to 20 minutes, or until potatoes are crisply tender and cheese has melted and browned lightly.
4. Sprinkle with red pepper and chervil before serving.

* If you like things hot, use red jalapeños or even serranos as substitutes for the bell pepper (some of the best peppers in the country are grown at Zillah, in the Yakima Valley).

Serves 4 to 6

Fresh Peas, Carrots, and Potatoes in Cream Sauce

Virginia Beck always takes advantage of the freshest seasonal produce available. Any vegetables she cannot grow herself she buys at one of our numerous farmers' markets.

Small carrots   8
Small new potatoes   8
Shelled peas   ½ cup
Milk   1 cup
Onion   1 thin slice
Parsley sprig   1
Unsalted butter (see Index)   2 tablespoons
Flour   2 tablespoons
Heavy cream   2 tablespoons
Nutmeg   dash
Cayenne   dash
Freshly ground white pepper and salt   to taste
Dry sherry   1 tablespoon

1. Peel and pare carrots and potatoes. Steam until almost tender. Add peas and steam another 2 minutes.
2. While vegetables are steaming, combine milk with onion and parsley and bring almost to a boil in a double boiler.
3. Melt butter and gently stir in flour with a wire whisk, making a smooth paste.
4. Strain hot milk mixture into butter/flour mixture and cream and stir vigorously with whisk. When mixture is thickened and smooth, simmer gently for 5 minutes, stirring occasionally. Add seasonings and sherry.
5. Combine vegetables and sauce and heat for a few minutes. Add a small amount of milk or cream if sauce is too thick. Serve.

Serves 4

Herbed Honey Carrots

This recipe calls for sweet, stubby carrots like Scarlet Nantes, Danvers Half-long, or Little Finger (if Little Fingers are very small, they may be used whole).

Carrots   1 pound, cut into ⅛-inch slices
Whole allspice   ¼ teaspoon
Unsalted butter (see Index)   2 tablespoons
Honey (try Cascara for its unusual flavor)   1 tablespoon
Grated lemon peel and juice   from 1 lemon
Lemon thyme   1 teaspoon chopped
Lemon slices   4, cut paper-thin

1. Cook carrots in water in covered saucepan with allspice until just tender (10 to 15 minutes); drain.
2. Add remaining ingredients to carrots in pan; heat well over low heat, stirring occasionally (do not burn). Divide into 4 portions, decorating each with 1 lemon slice. Serve hot.

Serves 4

Pasta with Vegetables

Unsalted butter (see Index)   6 tablespoons
Onion   2 tablespoons chopped
Flour   2 tablespoons
Light soy sauce   ½ teaspoon
Nutmeg   ½ teaspoon grated
Cream   1 cup
Fresh pasta (fettucine or linguine)   6 ounces
Carrots   2 cups, cut on the bias into 2-inch slices and cooked
Broccoli flowerets   2 cups cooked
Goat Cheddar, white extrasharp Cheddar, or Cascadian cheese   ¼ cup crumbled or grated

1. Melt butter in heavy cast-iron skillet. Add onion. Sauté until golden. Carefully stir in flour to make a roux. Cook for 3 minutes.
2. Add soy sauce and nutmeg, blending well; carefully stir in cream. Cook over medium heat, stirring continuously until sauce begins to bubble, about 8 to 10 minutes. Boil for 1 minute, being careful not to burn. Cook pasta, drain, and mix with sauce. Stir vegetables into pasta. Reduce heat to low and continue cooking until heated through (3 to 4 minutes).
3. Sprinkle with cheese just before serving.

Serves 6

Mama Sketti's Favorite Fettucine

This recipe, which takes full advantage of the Northwest's spring vegetable bounty, comes from Bellingham's Italian community (a sizeable and very vocal subculture). It's very tasty, provided your vegetables are fresh.

Dried fettucini noodles   12 ounces
Asparagus   ½ pound, tops only, sliced into 1-inch pieces
Mushrooms   ¼ pound
Small zucchini   2, sliced
Garlic cloves   2, crushed
Unsalted butter (see Index)   ½ cup
Whipping cream   1 cup
Parmesan cheese   ½ cup grated
Salt   1 teaspoon
Freshly ground white pepper   ¼ teaspoon

1. Cook fettucini according to package directions.
2. Meanwhile, sauté vegetables and garlic in butter until tender. Add remaining ingredients and cook until hot. Do not boil.
3. Pour over hot pasta, tossing to coat noodles. If desired, sprinkle additional parmesan on top.

Serves 6 (unless you're very hungry—in which case it serves 2)

Vegetable Medley

This is a quick and easy side dish that goes very well with a variety of meat dishes; or it may be used to stuff crêpes and served as a lunch.

Vegetable oil   2 tablespoons
Large carrots   2, coarsely grated
Small to medium zucchini   2, coarsely grated
Celery root*   one ½-inch slice, coarsely grated
Chives   2 to 3 tablespoons finely cut
Gingerroot   1 piece the size of a hazelnut; peeled and finely grated
Soy sauce   1 tablespoon
Mirin   1 tablespoon

Heat oil in pan until very hot. Add vegetables and turn heat to low. Cook for 2 to 3 minutes, until carrots are soft. Add soy sauce; stir to blend. Add mirin; stir to blend. Serve hot.

* You may substitute other vegetables, such as parsnip, turnip, daikon, or Japanese black radish, for the celery root.

Serves 4 to 6 (4 servings of 2 crêpes each if used for filling)

Cucumber Sauce

Serve over fish, crustaceans, shellfish, or vegetables.

Large Japanese cucumber   1
Light cream   ¼ cup
Rhubarb juice*   1 tablespoon strained
Watercress leaves   10, blanched
Crème fraîche (see Index)   1 cup
Salt   to taste
Hot paprika   dash
Rhubarb   1 teaspoon grated

1. Cut the cucumber into small pieces (peel and seed if an American cucumber is used).
2. Drop pieces into food processor work bowl (with steel blade) with the light cream, rhubarb juice, and watercress.
3. Agitate until cucumber is pureed and mixture is pale green.
4. Stir puree into crème fraîche with wire whisk in smooth, continuous motion.
5. Season with salt and paprika to taste; stir in grated rhubarb.

* To make rhubarb juice, squeeze cubed rhubarb through a garlic press.

Variation: If you don't like the oxalic acid taste of rhubarb, substitute lemon or lime juice for the rhubarb and rhubarb juice.

Makes 2 cups

Main
Courses

Spring Salmon with Spring Vegetables

There's something really special about that first fresh salmon each spring, a fish that is tasty and fat and juicy, quite unlike the frozen or imported salmon we've subsisted on over the winter. It's something that's eagerly awaited because there's nothing quite like it. And it goes exceptionally well with fresh spring vegetables. Accompany this dish with a new white wine from the previous fall's vintage—a dry semillon, sauvignon blanc, riesling, or even a white pinot noir.

Onion   1½ cups coarsely chopped
Celery   1½ cups thinly sliced on the diagonal
Heart of cattails   ½ cup thinly sliced on the diagonal
Unsalted butter (see Index)   2 tablespoons
Lettuce   2 cups shredded
Dill   1 teaspoon chopped
Nuoc mam   1 teaspoon
Salt and freshly ground black pepper   to taste
Salmon steaks   four, 6-ounces each
Dry pinot noir blanc   2 tablespoons
Sugar pea or sugar snap pea pods   1½ cups
Lemon wedges   4

1. Sauté onion, celery, and cattail hearts in butter for 5 minutes. Add lettuce, dill, nuoc mam, salt, and pepper; cook and stir 2 minutes over low heat.
2. Season salmon with salt and pepper. Place on top of vegetables in skillet. Add wine. Cook, covered, over low heat 10 to 15 minutes or until salmon flakes easily when tested with a fork. Remove to a platter; keep warm.
3. Add pea pods to vegetable mixture; cook and stir 3 or 4 minutes over medium heat or until pea pods are crisp and tender.
4. Arrange salmon over vegetables on warm platter; garnish with 1 lemon wedge per steak.

Serves 4

Mushroom Hazelnut Broiled Salmon Steaks

I love the taste of wild mushrooms, hazelnuts, and fresh salmon. It seems to be the gustatory essence of the Northwest. Accompany this dish with a crisp salad, topped with a cranberry dressing, and with fresh peas and boiled new potatoes. Serve this meal with a dry riesling or sauvignon blanc.

Salmon steaks   four, about ¾-inch thick each, approximately 1½ pounds total
Lemon juice and grated peel   from 1 lemon
Unsalted butter (see Index)   2 tablespoons, softened
Meadow mushrooms or commercial mushrooms   ½ pound, chopped
Parsley   2 tablespoons chopped
Hazelnuts   2 tablespoons sliced and toasted
Nuoc mam   ½ teaspoon
Lemon wedges   4
Parsley sprigs   4
Salmon caviar   2 teaspoons drained

1. Place fish on broiler grill and sprinkle with lemon juice. Broil 4 to 5 inches from heat for 4 to 5 minutes on each side or until fish flakes easily when prodded with fork.
2. Meanwhile, in bowl, combine butter and lemon peel. Stir in mushrooms, parsley, hazelnuts, and nuoc mam. Spoon mixture over fish steaks. Broil for 1 to 2 minutes longer.
3. Garnish with 1 lemon wedge, 1 parsley sprig, and ½ teaspoon salmon caviar per steak.

Serves 4

Garlic Broiled Salmon

My grandfather detested both the taste and smell of garlic, but he believed in a naturopath who convinced him he needed garlic to keep his somewhat dilapidated circulatory system going. So my frustrated grandpa ate garlic in the form of, strange to say, garlic pills—several times a day. Salmon is thought to lower blood cholesterol levels as well—so how can you go wrong with a dish like this. It's not only tasty, but it's good for you too. A good northwest sauvignon blanc should hold up nicely to the garlic; or try a first-rate lager beer.

Olive oil   ⅓ cup
Elephant garlic cloves   8, crushed in garlic press
Chervil   ¼ cup chopped
Dill   ½ teaspoon chopped
Nuoc mam   ½ teaspoon
Fine dry cracker or bread crumbs   1 cup
King salmon steaks   six, about 1-inch thick
Unsalted butter (see Index)   ¼ cup, softened

1. Process oil, garlic, chervil, dill, and nuoc mam in blender until smooth. Mix with cracker crumbs.
2. Place salmon on well-greased broiler rack; brush steaks with butter. Broil about 4 inches from heat for 8 to 10 minutes or until fish flakes easily when tested with a fork.
3. Carefully turn steaks. Spread about 2 tablespoons garlic mixture on each salmon steak. Return to broiler and broil 1 to 2 minutes more or until lightly browned. Serve hot.

Serves 6

Dill Broiled Salmon

Somehow the crisp, herby taste of dill seems to go very well with the flavor of fresh salmon, and I sometimes feel that the more dill there is in a salmon dish the better I like it. In this recipe, I have given what I consider to be a moderate amount of dill. If you feel this is too strong, reduce it; if you like your fish very dilly, increase it. Both the dill and the salmon should be very fresh.

White wine vinegar   2 tablespoons
Olive oil   3 tablespoons
Dill   1 tablespoon chopped
Medium sweet onion   1, cut into thick slices
King salmon steaks   6
Salt and freshly ground black pepper   to taste
Parsley   1 teaspoon chopped
Chives   1 teaspoon chopped
Lemon slices   6

1. Beat vinegar, oil, and dill to blend thoroughly. Add onion and let stand at room temperature at least 1 hour.
2. Remove onion, draining well.
3. Sprinkle both sides of salmon steaks with salt and pepper to taste. Beat oil mixture again. Dip fish into mixture and place on preheated, greased broiler rack. Broil about 2 inches from heat for 5 to 6 minutes, or until lightly browned. Baste with oil mixture and turn carefully. Brush uncooked side with mixture and broil 5 to 6 minutes longer, or until fish flakes easily when tested with a fork. Do not overcook fish or it will become tough.
4. Serve hot and garnish each serving with a sprinkling of parsley, chives, and a slice of lemon.

Serves 6

Salmon with Sorrel Sauce

This has become a seasonal favorite at La Petite Maison. It is Rick O'Reilly's variation of a recipe created by the Troisgros brothers of Roanne, France. It is a recipe that takes a little extra time because of the fish stock, but the final result is worth the trouble. Serve with a bone-dry sauvignon blanc or chardonnay.

Shallots   ¼ cup chopped
Dry white wine   1 cup
Fish stock (see Index)   1 cup
Heavy cream   1 cup
Salt   to taste
Freshly ground white pepper   ½ teaspoon
Sorrel   ¼ pound chopped
Unsalted butter (see Index)   as needed
Salmon scallops or very thin steaks   3 pounds

1. Place shallots and wine in a noncorrosive saucepan and boil until liquid is reduced by half. Strain out shallots, then add stock and cream to remaining liquid.
2. Reduce by half (boil down rapidly at this point); add salt and pepper.
3. Blanch sorrel in salted water. Drain. Add sorrel to sauce.
4. Melt butter in a skillet. Salt and pepper salmon scallops. Place in a skillet with hot butter. (Do not let them dry out; a few seconds to a minute, depending on the thickness of the slices, is enough to cook each side.)
5. Reheat sauce and pour over salmon. Use no garnish.

Serves 6

Chinook Salmon in Sorrel Sauce

Fresh shad can be substituted in this Sooke Harbour House recipe, but be very careful to remove the fine bones from the secondary bone structure and cook fillets for shorter time than salmon (exact cooking time will depend on thickness of fillets).

Unsalted butter (see Index)   1 tablespoon
Garlic glove   1, finely minced
Shallot   1, finely minced
Salmon fillets   two, 8 ounces each
Very dry white wine or vermouth   ½ cup
Fish stock (see Index)   ½ cup
Crème fraîche (see Index)   ¼ cup
Sorrel leaves   ⅔ cup thinly sliced

1. Melt butter in heavy skillet over high heat and sauté garlic and shallots. Add salmon fillets skin side up and sear for a maximum of 10 seconds. Turn fillets and add wine and stock. Lower heat to a simmer and cover skillet with foil. Cook for approximately 2 or 3 minutes, depending upon thickness of fillets. Remove fillets and keep warm.
2. Return skillet to high heat; with a wooden spoon stir crème fraîche and sorrel into pan liquids.
3. Place salmon on serving plates. When sauce reaches a creamy consistency, pour over salmon fillets and serve.

Serves 2

Salmon in Cranberry Vinegar Sauce

Sinclair Philip of the Sooke Harbour House believes in using as many native ingredients in his cookery as possible. Here's such a dish. Accompany this dish with a pinot noir blanc or an off-dry sauvignon blanc.

Unsalted butter (see Index)   4 tablespoons, clarified
Small garlic clove   1, finely minced
Small shallot   1, finely minced
Salmon fillets   two, 8 ounces each
Cranberry vinegar*   3 tablespoons
Fish stock (see Index)   1 cup
Unsalted butter (see Index)   ½ cup, room temperature

1. Preheat oven to 425°. Pour clarified butter, garlic, and shallots into a skillet with an oven-proof handle. Add salmon; sauté fillets quickly on 1 side. Turn fillets, add vinegar and stock and sauté quickly—for less than 30 seconds. Cover skillet with foil and bake in oven until fish is cooked, about 5 to 10 minutes. (The time will vary according to thickness of fillet.) Remove fish from pan and keep warm.
2. Reduce remaining liquids to ⅓. Incorporate ½ cup butter with wire whip. Arrange salmon on plate; cover with sauce.

* To make cranberry vinegar, place cranberries in a ceramic bowl, crush, and cover with rice vinegar. Cover bowl, put into a cool place, leaving a small opening to let vinegar "breathe." Let sit for 1 or 2 weeks. Strain and bottle.

Serves 1 or 2

Poached Salmon with Dill Sauce

In the summer, when it gets quite warm, Victoria and I don't much feel like cooking during the heat of the afternoon. We prefer sitting by the lake, sipping a chilled white or sparkling wine and nibbling on chilled food that has been prepared ahead of time. Here's one of our favorites.

Salmon   4 to 5 pounds, poached or smoked
Lettuce leaves   as needed
Chinese cabbage   3 to 4 cups shredded
Scallions   1½ to 2 cups shredded
Ripe tomatoes   1½ to 2, thinly sliced
English cucumber   1, thinly sliced
Enokitake mushrooms   garnish
Dill Sauce
Golden whitefish or red salmon caviar   3 to 4 teaspoons

1. Place salmon on beds of lettuce leaves filled with shredded cabbage and scallions (divide salmon into portions of ½ to ¾ pound per serving).
2. On each plate, just above salmon, place a strip of alternating tomato and cucumber slices. Tuck a small bunch of enokitake under each end of strips.
3. Top salmon with sauce; top sauce with ½ teaspoon caviar per serving.

Serves 4

Dill Sauce

Sour cream (see Index)   1 cup
White wine vinegar   2 tablespoons
Dill   1 to 2 tablespoons very finely minced
Salt and freshly ground white pepper   to taste

Combine all ingredients; chill well and serve over chilled salmon.

Makes 1⅓ to 1½ cups

Cold Salmon in Cucumber Sauce

This is a great dish for a hot summer day, when you're looking for something cool to eat. Serve with a variety of dipping vegetables like cherry tomatoes, cauliflower or broccoli florets, carrot sticks, green pepper strips, and cooked asparagus tips. Accompany with a well-chilled sauvignon blanc or premium lager beer.

Salmon fillets   2, poached or smoked
Lemon juice   1 tablespoon
Cucumber Sauce   2½ cups

1. Brush fillets lightly with lemon juice; let chill in refrigerator for several hours.
2. Remove fillets onto serving platter, ladle sauce over fish, or let your guests use sauce as a dip for salmon chunks and vegetables.

Allow ¼ to ½ pound of fish per serving

Cucumber Sauce

Heavy cream   1 cup
Cream cheese (see Index)   2 tablespoons
Dill   2 teaspoons chopped
Green onion   1 tablespoon finely chopped, green portion only
Chervil or parsley   1 teaspoon snipped or minced
Lemon juice   ¼ to ½ teaspoon
Salt and freshly ground white pepper   to taste
Japanese cucumber   ¼ cup diced, plus 1 tablespoon

1. Slowly heat cream and cream cheese in double boiler. Add dill, onion, chervil, lemon juice; season with salt and pepper.
2. Mash 1 tablespoon cucumber; save juice. Remove cream mixture from heat, cool, and add cucumber juice and remaining cucumber. Blend well. Chill sauce well in refrigerator until it thickens.

Makes 1½ cups

Cold Poached Salmon with Sunomono Dressing

Cold poached salmon is a summer favorite throughout the Northwest. The following recipe adds an interesting twist to this popular warm-weather dish. Accompany this salmon with rice and steamed buttered vegetables and a well-chilled northwest sauvignon blanc (or even a big chardonnay). If the weather is very warm, enjoy it with cold lager beer.

Whole salmon, head and tail on   one, 3½ to 4 pounds
Dry sauvignon blanc   1 cup
Rice vinegar   ½ cup
Water   3 cups
Onion   ¼ cup chopped
Lovage or celery   ¼ cup chopped
Nuoc mam   ½ teaspoon
Lemon thyme   ¼ teaspoon chopped
Bay leaf   1
Japanese cucumber   1
Sunomono Dressing
Horseradish Soy Sauce
Thin lemon slices   12 to 16
Live crawfish   12 to 16 (optional)
Salmon caviar   6 to 8 teaspoons drained

1. Place fish on greased rack in fish poacher. Add wine, vinegar, water, onion, lovage, nuoc mam, thyme, and bay leaf. Bring to a boil; reduce heat to low. Cover and poach 20 to 25 minutes, or until fish flakes easily when tested with a fork. Remove pan from heat; allow salmon to cool slightly in poaching liquid, 15 to 20 minutes.
2. Remove salmon from poacher (reserve liquid for fish chowder). Carefully peel off skin with very sharp knife, leaving head and tail intact. Transfer fish to a large serving platter. (I like to place it on a bed of well-scrubbed cattail leaves.)
3. While fish is cooling, finely slice cucumber and soak in salted water (2 tablespoons salt to 1 quart water) for 15 minutes. Squeeze to drain. Cucumber slices should be limp.
4. Make dressings.
5. Garnish salmon with lemon slices; surround base of salmon with overlapping, scalelike strip of cucumber slices. Pour Sunomono Dressing over salmon and cucumber slices—just enough to bathe flesh and moisten cucumber slices.
6. Kill crawfish by twisting tails from bodies. Shell tails, leaving end fins attached to meat; remove sand veins running down top of tails (use caution: raw crawfish meat is much more delicate than the cooked tail). Place tails, fins out, in 2 rows on top of cucumber slices, 1 row to each side of salmon.
7. Serve immediately. Carefully pour more Sunomono Dressing over fish.
8. Give each guest a small bowl of Horseradish Soy Sauce. Start meal by picking up crawfish by tail, dipping into sauce, and eating them (there should be at least 2 crawfish per guest). Then portion out salmon.

Serves 6 to 8

Sunomono Dressing *(Sanbaizu)*

Hon-mirin 1½ tablespoons
Rice vinegar ½ cup
Light soy sauce 2 tablespoons
Water ½ to ⅔ cup

Mix all ingredients in saucepan over medium heat; use water to adjust acidity to your liking. Bring to a boil, remove from heat, and cool to room temperature.

Makes 1 to 1⅓ cups

Horseradish Soy Sauce

Mix 1 tablespoon finely grated wasabi root or wasabi powder with ½ cup dark soy sauce.

Makes ½ cup

Sautéed Spring Salmon with Spring Vegetables

This is a nice way to prepare the early spring run of king salmon, which comes at about the time the first fresh northwest asparagus is available. Or use tender bracken shoots. Accompany this dish with a dry chardonnay or other white wine.

King salmon steaks four, 4 to 6 ounces each
Salt and freshly ground black pepper to taste
Vegetable oil 6 tablespoons
Green onion ¼ cup chopped
Nuoc mam 1 teaspoon
Thyme ½ teaspoon chopped
Asparagus 1½ cups diagonally sliced into 1-inch pieces
Shiitake or oyster mushrooms 1½ cups
Cold water ¼ cup
Lemon peel or gingerroot 1 teaspoon grated
Lemon slices 4

1. Season salmon with salt and pepper. Sauté in 4 tablespoons oil until browned on both sides. Allow 10 minutes cooking time per inch of thickness measured at the thickest part.
2. In separate skillet, heat 2 tablespoons oil. Add onion, nuoc mam, and thyme; sauté 30 seconds. Add asparagus, mushrooms, water, and lemon peel; cover and simmer 2 minutes or until vegetables are crisp-tender.
3. Place salmon steaks on serving platter. Remove vegetables with slotted spoon and place around salmon steaks. Garnish salmon with lemon slices.

Serves 4

Poached King Salmon with Tarragon Sauce

This is a pleasant cool treat for a hot summer day. The salmon may be cooked ahead of time and refrigerated until use. Accompany this dish with a chilled chardonnay, dry riesling, or Château Benoit brut sparkling wine.

King salmon   4 to 5 pounds
Lager beer   2¼ cups
Tarragon sprigs   2
Onion   2 tablespoons minced
Lovage or celery   1 teaspoon finely chopped
Whole black peppercorns   4
Nuoc mam or salt   ½ teaspoon
Freshly ground black pepper   to taste
Tarragon Sauce

1. Place salmon in fish poacher or on rack in large roasting pan.
2. Combine beer and seasonings; pour over fish. Cover and simmer over very low heat for 45 minutes. Baste occasionally with cooking liquid.
3. Carefully lift salmon from pan and remove skin.
4. Divide into individual servings or keep whole and place on a bed of fresh lettuce leaves. Chill and serve with Tarragon Sauce.

Serves 6 to 8

Tarragon Sauce

Sour cream (see Index)   1 cup
Green onions   1 tablespoon minced
White tarragon vinegar   2 tablespoons
Tarragon   1 teaspoon finely chopped
Salt and freshly ground white pepper   to taste

Combine all ingredients; chill well and serve over salmon.

Makes 1 cup

Fettucine with Smoked Salmon

The Osteria Mitchelli, a pleasant restaurant overlooking Lake Union in Seattle, specializes in fresh seafood, but also serves a number of other specialties, including smoked salmon. This northwest delicacy is presented in a number of different ways. Here is a particularly tasty one. I found that Grant's Imperial Russian Stout goes very well with this dish.

Unsalted butter (see Index)   2 tablespoons
Shallots   1 tablespoon minced
Hard-smoked salmon   6 ounces, cubed
Scotch whiskey   ¼ cup
Heavy cream   1½ cups
Shelled peas   1 cup, cooked
Fresh fettucine   1 pound

1. Melt butter in saucepan; add shallots and cook 2 minutes over medium heat. Add salmon; cook 2 minutes. Add whiskey and cover pan so it does not ignite. Cook 2 more minutes. Add cream. Cook 15 minutes, stirring occasionally. Add peas just before serving.
2. Meanwhile, cook pasta. Toss with sauce and serve immediately.

Serves 2 to 4

Ray's Boathouse Summer Salmon Barbecue

Ray's Boathouse consistently serves the freshest fish of any restaurant in Seattle. Here's one of their favorite ways of barbecuing fresh salmon.

Soy sauce   1 quart
Brown sugar   1 pound
Dry mustard   1 tablespoon
Whole cloves   2, freshly crushed
Gingerroot   1 tablespoon chopped
White wine   ½ cup
Salmon fillets   six, about 8 ounces each
Toasted sesame seeds

1. Prepare marinade by combining all ingredients except salmon and sesame seeds.
2. Place fillets in marinade and allow to marinate 4 to 6 hours.
3. Broil salmon on a barbecue grill until done, about 7 to 10 minutes. Top with toasted seasame seeds.

Serves 6

Oven-Baked Trout

This recipe calls for freshly caught trout. Pond-raised trout that has been on a supermarket cooler shelf for a few days and turned soft or developed off-flavors is not an adequate substitute. Accompany this dish with a bone-dry chardonnay or riesling.

Rainbow or cutthroat trout   1
Small onion   1 per pound of fish
Small ripe tomato   1 per pound of fish
Country or home-cured bacon strips   2
Unsalted butter (see Index)   2 teaspoons, softened

1. Bleed and clean trout, leaving head on. Rinse cavity well.
2. Slice onion and tomato. Line cavity with slices—onion on the outside, tomato on the inside, and bacon strips in the center. Dab with butter and wrap in foil.
3. Bake in 400° degree oven until done (allow 10 minutes for every inch of thickness).

Serves 1 (or more, if you catch the big "un")

Truite au Beurre Rouge (Stuffed Trout with Salmon and Red Butter Sauce)

I first enjoyed this dish at a luncheon at Seattle's foremost French restaurant, Le Tastevin, and liked it so much I asked owners Jacques Boiroux and Emile Ninaud for the recipe. It is delicious and, despite its French name, it is very northwest.

Trout   six, 8 ounces each, boned
Salmon Mousse   6 tablespoons
Beurre Rouge   2 cups
Lemon slices   garnish
Watercress   garnish

1. Stuff trout with approximately 1 tablespoon of the Salmon Mousse each. Slowly poach or steam trout for 15 to 20 minutes.
2. Transfer trout to serving platter and remove skins; spoon some Beurre Rouge sauce over fish. Serve remaining sauce on the side.
3. Garnish platter with lemon wheels and watercress bouquets.

Serves 6

Salmon Mousse

Salmon fillet   ½ pound, skinned
Large egg white   1
Heavy cream   1 cup
Cayenne pepper and salt   to taste

Chop fish to a smooth puree in a food processor using the metal blade. Add egg white and heavy cream in a slow stream. Season to taste with a pinch of cayenne and a little salt. Refrigerate mousse for 1 hour before using.

Makes 1¼ to 1½ cups

Beurre Rouge

Red wine   ½ cup
Shallots   2, very finely chopped
Cayenne pepper   pinch
Heavy cream   ¼ cup
Unsalted butter (see Index)   ¾ pound, cut into small pieces

In a heavy stainless steel or enameled saucepan, boil wine with shallots and cayenne until approximately 2 ounces of liquid remain. Add cream, boil for 5 more minutes, and then whisk butter pieces a few at a time into sauce, until sauce has a creamy consistency. Remove from heat as soon as all butter has been incorporated.

Makes 2¼ cups

Rainbow Trout Soufflé

This recipe is, of course, best if the fish has been caught earlier on the day on which the soufflé is prepared. Small kokanee may be used instead of rainbow trout. Accompany this dish with an Oregon chardonnay or with a Château Benoit or Hinzerling sparkling wine.

Trout   four, 8 ounces each
Egg whites 4
Nuoc mam or salt   ½ teaspoon
Freshly ground white pepper   ¼ teaspoon
Nutmeg   pinch
Whipping cream   1½ cups
Unsalted butter (see Index)   2 tablespoons, melted
Paprika   ½ teaspoon
Lemon-Butter Sauce
Chervil or parsley   4 teaspoons finely chopped
Lemon slices 4
Steelhead caviar   4 teaspoons

1. With a very sharp knife, carefully remove flesh from fish, leaving head, tail, and skin intact and connected. Thoroughly bone meat; pick over by hand and remove tiny bones with tweezers. Put boned meat through grinder. In food processor work bowl fitted with steel blade, combine egg whites, nuoc mam, pepper, and nutmeg with ground fish; beat until a smooth paste has formed. Add cream; beat with pulsating motion until mixture begins to thicken, then increase speed and beat until mixture resembles dough.
2. Stuff ¼ of mixture into each trout skin, shaping it to resemble the shape of the original fish as closely as possible. Place stuffed trout in greased pan. Brush with butter and lightly sprinkle with paprika. Bake in 450° oven for 15 minutes. Trout will puff up.
3. Remove trout from oven. Place on serving platter or on individual serving plates. Pour sauce over trout; sprinkle with chervil and place 1 lemon slice in center of each trout. Drop a teaspoon of caviar on top of each lemon slice.

Serves 4

Lemon-Butter Sauce

Unsalted butter (see Index)   4 tablespoons
Large, very ripe tomato   1, cooked, peeled, and pureed
Lemon juice   3 tablespoons

In small saucepan, melt butter; let cool. Pour off clear top layer and save; discard solids in bottom. Return clear portion to saucepan; heat slowly until light brown. Add tomato puree and lemon juice, heat through. Pour over fish.

Poached Smoked Cod

This is a recipe from British Columbia's large Scottish community. Try it as an unusual breakfast treat.

Smoked cod fillets   2
Milk   1 cup (or more, as needed)
Unsalted butter (see Index)   2 tablespoons, melted
Toast

1. Place fillets in large saucepan. Pour in milk to cover fillets.
2. Slowly bring milk to a boil (make sure not to burn milk—use a double boiler if necessary). Simmer for 20 minutes.
3. Flake fillets and serve with melted butter over toast.

Note: Do not add salt, since the smoked fillets are already salted.

Serves 2

Baked Smoked Cod

Here's a recipe for those cold winter nights when you're sitting in your snug beach cabin while the wind lashes the surf to a froth. This hearty dish is best accompanied by a jug of stout ale (Redhook or Grant's) or by some hot, spicy mulled wine.

Small smoked cod fillets   8
Cream or milk   2 cups (or more, as needed)
Unsalted butter (see Index)   2 tablespoons
Freshly ground white pepper   ¼ teaspoon
Medium onion   1, chopped

1. Place fillets in baking dish. Pour in cream until fillets are partly covered.
2. Add butter, pepper, and onion.
3. Bake in moderate oven at 350° for 40 minutes.

Serves 8

Sole in Fresh Lemon Butter

The fish used in this recipe must be absolutely fresh; otherwise, it may develop an unpleasant side taste. The same goes for the shrimp—there should be no iodine off-taste. Accompany this dish with a very crisp northwest chardonnay.

Small shrimp   ½ cup chopped
Dry bread crumbs   ½ cup
Unsalted butter (see Index)   6 tablespoons, melted
Nuoc mam   ½ teaspoon
Lemon juice   1 teaspoon
Chervil   1 teaspoon finely chopped
Sorrel leaves   1 teaspoon finely chopped
Garden orache   1 teaspoon finely chopped (optional)
Sole fillets   four, ¼ pound each
Lemon Butter
Salmon caviar   2 teaspoons drained

1. Preheat oven to 350°.
2. In small bowl, stir together first 8 ingredients. Place 2 tablespoons mixture at large end of each fillet. Roll up fillet; secure with wooden skewer.
3. Place rolls in flat glass or ceramic baking pan; pour Lemon Butter over fish.
4. Bake for 20 to 25 minutes, or until fish flakes easily.
5. After placing fish on serving platter, decorate each serving with ½ teaspoon salmon caviar.

Serves 4

Lemon Butter

Unsalted butter (see Index)   2 tablespoons, melted
Lemon juice   1 teaspoon

Blend together butter and lemon juice. Pour over fish.

Makes ⅛ cup

Sole with Oyster Mushrooms in White Wine Sauce

Sole is a very light and delicate fish. It goes very well with delicate oyster mushrooms, now available on a regular basis as cultivated mushrooms. Both sole and oyster mushrooms are easily overpowered by strong condiments and spices, but lend themselves to enhancement by simple, flavorful sauces. Accompany this dish with a dry northwest sauvignon blanc or semillon.

Unsalted butter (see Index)   2 tablespoons
Oyster mushrooms   ½ pound, sliced
Gingerroot   one 1-inch chunk, smashed with a cleaver
Sole fillets   six, 6 to 8 ounces each
Salt and freshly ground white pepper   to taste
Dry sauvignon blanc   ½ cup
Small shrimp   ½ pound cooked
White Wine Sauce

1. Melt butter in large cast-iron skillet or electric frying pan and add mushrooms. Place smashed ginger into garlic press and squeeze juice into pan. Brown mushrooms very lightly. Skim mushrooms from pan; set aside.
2. Season each fillet with salt and pepper and fold each fillet in half, tail to head. Arrange in single layer in skillet. Add wine; cover, and poach over low heat until fish flakes easily, about 10 minutes.
3. Carefully lift fish from pan to hot platter. Boil pan juices rapidly, uncovered, until reduced to ⅓ original volume. Stir reduced broth, mushrooms, and shrimp into White Wine Sauce. Heat thoroughly and pour over hot fish.

Serves 6

White Wine Sauce

Unsalted butter (see Index)   3 tablespoons
Shallots   2, finely chopped
Flour   2 teaspoons
Dry sauvignon blanc   ½ cup
Cream   1 cup
Salt and freshly ground white pepper   to taste

1. Melt butter in heavy skillet. Add shallots and cook until lightly browned. Carefully stir in flour to make a roux.
2. Add wine, stir, and add cream. Blend well. Cook, stirring, until thickened. Season to taste with salt and pepper. Simmer 10 minutes to burn off alcohol and to blend flavors.

Makes 1½ cups

Hazelnut Halibut

I like hazelnuts so much, I can eat them with anything, from appetizers to desserts. Here's one of my favorite hazelnut/fish main dishes; it goes well with a dry or off-dry sauvignon blanc, or even with a fruity riesling.

Halibut steaks   four, 6 ounces each
Salt and freshly ground black pepper   to taste
Hazelnuts   6 tablespoons finely ground
Unsalted butter (see Index)   4 tablespoons, melted
Lemon juice   4 teaspoons

1. Season halibut with salt and pepper.
2. Combine hazelnuts and butter. Spread ⅓ of mixture into bottom of shallow baking dish. Place halibut on nuts. Top with remaining butter mixture. Sprinkle with lemon juice.
3. Bake in a preheated 350° oven for 25 to 30 minutes or until halibut flakes easily when tested with a fork.

Serves 4

Steamed Flounder Fillets with Chervil Butter

All of the "sole" found in the Pacific Northwest are actually flounders, but that makes them no less tasty than true sole. Accompany this dish with a dry northwest chardonnay, sauvignon blanc, semillon, or a well-chilled northwest premium lager beer.

Thin flounder fillets   eight, about 2 pounds total
Unsalted butter (see Index)   6 tablespoons, melted
Lemon juice   3 tablespoons
Nuoc mam   1 teaspoon
Freshly ground white pepper   ½ teaspoon
Onion   2 tablespoons minced
Lovage or celery   ¼ cup minced
Lemon thyme   ½ teaspoon minced
Dry bread crumbs   2 cups
Chervil Butter

1. Marinate fish for 20 minutes in mixture of 4 tablespoons butter, 2 tablespoons lemon juice, ½ teaspoon nuoc mam, and ¼ teaspoon pepper.
2. Sauté onion and lovage in remaining 2 tablespoons butter. Add ½ teaspoon nuoc mam, ¼ teaspoon pepper, 1 tablespoon lemon juice, thyme, and bread crumbs. Cook until crumbs have absorbed liquid.
3. Place ⅛ of mixture on wide end of each fillet; roll up and hold in place with a well-soaked bamboo skewer.
4. Lay fillet rolls into bottom of steamer basket. Place basket over vigorously boiling water.

Steam for about 8 to 10 minutes, or until fish is just done.
5. Place fillets on serving platter; cover with hot Chervil Butter.

Serves 4 to 6

Chervil Butter

Unsalted butter (see Index)   ½ cup
Lemon juice   2 tablespoons
Lime juice   2 tablespoons
Chervil   4 tablespoons finely chopped
Lime rind   1 teaspoon grated
Lemon rind   1 teaspoon grated
Nuoc mam   ½ teaspoon
Freshly ground white pepper   ¼ teaspoon

Melt butter and beat in lemon and lime juice; stir in remaining ingredients. Pour over whitefish or chicken while hot.

Makes 1 cup

Sand Dabs in Chervil Butter Sauce

The sand dab is a small founderlike bottom fish common on the West Coast. Like sole, it should be absolutely fresh and come from unpolluted waters to be at its best. This dish goes well with boiled potatoes, steamed vegetables, and a dry Oregon chardonnay.

Sand dabs   8
Salt and freshly ground pepper   to taste
Flour   as needed
Unsalted butter (see Index)   8 tablespoons
Chervil   ¼ cup minced
Steelhead caviar   4 teaspoons
Lemon wedges   8

1. Clean fresh dabs, removing head and tail. Large dabs should be filleted. Sprinkle with salt and pepper and dredge lightly in flour.
2. In heavy cast-iron skillet, heat 4 tablespoons butter until just below sizzling. Add fish, a couple at a time, and cook quickly until lightly browned (if butter becomes too dark during cooking, replace with a new batch). Remove cooked dabs to warm platter and cook remaining fish, adding butter as needed.
3. When all fish are cooked, add 2 tablespoons butter to drippings in pan and heat until bubbly. Pour over fish. Sprinkle fish with chervil. Garnish each with ½ teaspoon caviar and 1 lemon wedge.

Serves 8

Grilled Rockfish Steaks

Any large rockfish may be used for this recipe. Serve with roasted potatoes, steamed winter vegetables, and a dry to medium-dry riesling or gewürztraminer.

Red rockfish steaks   four to six, about 2 pounds total
Lemon juice   ¼ cup
Olive oil or vegetable oil   ½ cup
Pure sesame oil   1 teaspoon
Dry sherry   ¼ cup
Mushroom soy sauce   ½ tablespoon
Nuoc mam   2 teaspoons
Freshly ground white pepper   ¼ teaspoon
Onion   ¼ cup finely grated
Hot paprika   ¼ teaspoon

1. Place steaks inside wire fish cooking grill and set about 4 inches over hot barbecue coals.
2. Make sauce from remaining ingredients, except paprika.
3. Baste fish with ½ of sauce, then sprinkle with ½ of paprika. Cook for about 8 minutes; baste, turn, and baste again with remaining sauce and sprinkle with remaining paprika. Cook 7 to 10 minutes longer or until flesh turns opaque and flakes easily. Serve hot.

Serves 4 to 6

Rockfish with Cream Sauce

Any of the many species of rockfish common to our waters may be used in this recipe. To assure good taste, however, the fish must be absolutely fresh and it should have been handled properly. Select only fillets that are free from fishy odors, and avoid any that have reddish flesh (this indicates improper bleeding). This dish goes well with a number of northwest white wines: try it with a dry chardonnay, a very dry riesling, or a fruity sauvignon blanc or semillon.

Salt and freshly ground black pepper   ¼ teaspoon each
Thyme   1 teaspoon finely chopped
Lemon juice   1 tablespoon
Whole rockfish   one, about 3 pounds, cleaned
Olive oil   2 tablespoons
Lemon thyme   ½ teaspoon finely chopped
Cream Sauce

1. Combine salt, pepper, thyme, and lemon juice. Rub mixture inside fish cavity. Rub outside of fish with olive oil and sprinkle with lemon thyme.
2. Place fish in greased baking pan. Bake in 350° oven for 45 to 60 minutes, until fish flakes easily. Pour Cream Sauce over fish and serve.

Serves 2 to 4

Cream Sauce

Shallots   ¼ cup finely chopped
Small garlic clove   1, crushed
White wine vinegar   ¼ cup
Sauvignon blanc   ¼ cup
Whipping cream   1½ cups

1. In small heavy pan, combine shallots, garlic, vinegar, and wine. Bring to a boil; cook until reduced to 3 tablespoons.
2. Strain and discard solids.
3. In a heavy 3-quart saucepan, boil cream gently until reduced to ¾ cup. Add strained wine liquid. Blend well and serve over fish.

Makes slightly less than 1 cup

Carp Braised in Chicken Fat

Carp are common in many of the lakes east of the Cascades, but few people fish for them. But they are quite easy to catch and good to eat when they are impeccably fresh. If you do not angle, you can find live (or at least very fresh) carp at Chinese fish markets. The flavor of this dish does not go well with wine; accompany it with a good beer instead.

Garlic cloves   4, finely minced
Lemon juice   1 teaspoon
Lemon peel   ½ teaspoon grated
Green onions   4, cut into 1-inch lengths
Carp   one, about 3 pounds, cleaned and scaled
Salt   1 teaspoon
Chicken fat   ¼ cup
Chinese chili sauce   2 tablespoons
Oyster sauce   3 tablespoons
Chicken stock (see Index)   as needed (enough to cover fish, about 6 to 8 cups)
Soy sauce   2 tablespoons
Tofu   2 cakes, cut into 1- by 1- by ½-inch pieces.

1. Combine garlic, lemon juice and peel, and onions. Set aside.
2. Sprinkle carp with salt and rub salt well into skin.
3. Heat chicken fat in skillet; add chili sauce, oyster sauce, and garlic/lemon/onion mixture.
4. When skillet is extremely hot, place fish in skillet and brown on both sides. Add enough stock to barely cover fish. Cover skillet and simmer for about 10 minutes or until fish is done.
5. Carefully remove fish and place on serving platter. Keep warm.
6. Season sauce with soy sauce. Add tofu and boil for 10 to 15 minutes. Arrange tofu pieces around fish and pour hot sauce over fish and tofu. Serve immediately.

Serves 4 to 6

Cabezon and Vegetable Kabobs

Accompany this dish with a dry white wine or a premium lager beer.

Olive oil   ½ cup
Lemon juice   3 tablespoons
Nuoc mam   1 teaspoon
Freshly ground black pepper   to taste
Bay leaf   1
Shallots   1 tablespoon finely chopped
Cabezon   2 to 2½ pounds, cut into 1-inch cubes
Thin Japanese cucumber   1, cut into ½-inch rounds
Ripe cherry tomatoes   12
Thin leeks or small onions   1 or 2, cut into ½-inch rounds
Olive oil   ½ cup

1. Mix together first 6 ingredients. Blend well. Add fish, making sure all pieces are covered well. Marinate for at least 2 hours.
2. Remove fish from marinade; pat dry and alternate fish and vegetables on 6 skewers. Brush each serving with a thin film of remaining olive oil. Broil kabobs 4 inches from charcoal for 5 to 10 minutes, turning skewers and basting often with olive oil.

Variations: Other white-meated, firm-fleshed fish can be used in this dish. Small fish like tomcod or pile perch can be cleaned and cut crosswise into sections with the skin left on. (If you use blennies or pricklebacks, soak them first for a couple of hours in a solution of 4 parts salt water to 1 part vinegar. Use garlic instead of the shallot called for in the recipe, then proceed as for cabezon.)

Serves 6

Poached Lamprey on Toast

Lampreys were much more esteemed as food in the past than they are now: northwest Indians processed these tasty fish by smoking, sun drying, and salting. There's a good reason for eating lampreys: the voracious critters prey on other fish. A few years ago, lampreys wiped out most of the fish in the Great Lakes—it's too bad no one thought of marketing the suddenly plentiful lampreys. But our final culinary determinant here has to do with taste, not with ecological impact. Lampreys are well worth searching out and eating.

Medium lamprey   1
Vegetable Fondue
Sauvignon blanc   2 cups (or more, as needed)
Salt and freshly ground black pepper   to taste
Garlic clove   1, minced
Parlsey   2 tablespoons finely chopped
Thyme sprig   1
Bay leaf   1
Small toast rounds
Unsalted butter (see Index)   1 tablespoon
Flour   1 tablespoon

1. Scald lamprey, then scrape off skin. Remove central nerve by cutting off tip of tail, making an incision around the neck below the body holes (a special lamprey feature whose purpose is unknown) and pulling out the nerve through this hole. Bleed and gut lamprey (no boning is necessary, since this eellike fish has none). Reserve roe. Cut body of lamprey into 1-inch sections (discard head and tail).
2. Place lamprey sections in heavy pan on top of Vegetable Fondue. Cover with wine; season with salt and pepper. Add garlic and herbs. Bring to a boil; cover pan; reduce heat and poach fish for 25 to 30 minutes. Drain lamprey pieces and arrange on toast rounds.
3. In meantime, gently poach roe in lightly salted water; remove when firm. Slice and place on top of lamprey sections.
4. Remove bay leaf from pan. Boil down pan juices until reduced by half. Make roux from butter and flour; stir into pan juices to make sauce. Pour sauce over fish and roe. Serve immediately, so toast does not get soggy.

Serves 4 to 6 as main course; 10 to 12 as appetizer

Vegetable Fondue

Unsalted butter (see Index)   4 tablespoons
Zucchini   4 tablespoons grated
Carrot   2 tablespoons grated
Onion   2 tablespoons grated
Leeks   1 tablespoon finely chopped, white part only
Celery   1 tablespoon finely chopped
Sorrel leaves   1 tablespoon finely sliced
Garden orache   1 tablespoon finely sliced

Cook all ingredients slowly over low heat until vegetables have been reduced to a pulp, stirring frequently to avoid sticking and burning.

Makes 1 cup

Sautéed Giant Acorn Barnacles

Sinclair Philip of Sooke Harbour House calls the giant barnacle one of the nicest seafoods in the Pacific Northwest, because it has the consistency of crab meat and scallop and a crablike flavor. Accompany barnacle with a nice, dry northwest chardonnay, sauvignon blanc, or riesling.

Unsalted butter (see Index)   2 tablespoons
Garlic   ⅛ teaspoon finely minced
Shallot   ⅛ teaspoon finely minced
Dry white wine   1 teaspoon
Giant barnacles*   4, cleaned and picked over (for shell pieces)
Parsley   ½ teaspoon finely chopped

In a small pan, melt butter over medium heat. Add garlic, shallot, and wine. Cook for a few seconds. Add barnacle meat and cook on both sides for approximately 5 seconds each. Add parsley and serve.

* To prepare the barnacles, break the shell with a hammer and remove the meat. Separate the roe from the flesh.

Serves 2

Marinated Seafood with Lamb's-Lettuce

The seafood for this Sooke Harbour House recipe must be very fresh. Accompany this dish with a dry northwest chardonnay or riesling.

Abalone   1
Rock scallop meat and roe   from 1
Salmon   8 ounces
Giant acorn barnacles   2, cleaned
Shallots   2 tablespoons finely chopped
Green peppercorns   2 tablespoons
Walnut oil   as needed (to cover seafood)
Green mustard or Dijon-style mustard   1 tablespoon
Apple cider vinegar   2 tablespoons
Walnut oil   8 tablespoons
Lamb's-lettuce   8 cups
Red bell pepper   ½, julienned
Lemon peel   from 1 lemon, blanched and julienned

1. Cut abalone and rock scallop muscles into almost transparent slices. Slice salmon thinly. Break up scallop roe into chunks. Place barnacle meat and other seafood in a porcelain container and cover with shallots, peppercorns, and walnut oil. Macerate for 15 minutes.
2. Blend mustard, vinegar, and 8 tablespoons walnut oil with a whisk.
3. Remove seafood from marinade. Drain and toss with lamb's-lettuce and vinaigrette. Decorate with bell pepper and lemon strips.

Serves 4

Fresh Sea Cucumber with Nuoc Mam and Fish Sauce Sooke Harbour House

The white, internal muscles of sea cucumbers are among our most delicately flavored marine foods. They should never be overcooked or overpowered by strong sauces. Accompany sea cucumber with a dry Oregon or Washington sauvignon blanc, chardonnay, or riesling.

Sea cucumber* 2 ounces
Fish stock (see Index) 2 tablespoons
Nuoc mam ¼ teaspoon
Leek ½ tablespoon very thinly sliced into rounds, white and green portions
Hazelnuts 3, quartered and slivered
Medium red bell pepper ⅛, julienned into ½-inch-long strips

Rinse sea cucumber under cold water. Let drain. Put stock and nuoc mam into frying pan at high heat. When liquid reaches boil, add sea cucumber, hazelnuts, leek, and pepper. Cook at high heat for approximately 1 minute, until liquid is nearly evaporated. Do not overcook: overcooking renders sea cucumber gummy and tough. Serve hot.

* As soon a possible after sea cucumber is taken from water, remove the 5 white internal muscles by hand or with a dull knife (a sharp knife will cut into muscle, making removal harder). The longer you wait, the limper (and thus more difficult to remove) the muscles become. Cut lengthwise between the 5 muscles to separate them; then cut them into ½-inch pieces. Cleaning a sea cucumber may stain your hands brown for 24 hours, so wash hands regularly during process or wear gloves.

Serves 1

Stir-Fried Spicy Frog Legs

Neither the bullfrog nor the green frog are native to the Northwest, but they have been introduced widely throughout our region. The green frog, the tastier and smaller of the two, is now very common along the lower reaches of the Fraser River. It's hard to tell who likes frog legs better—the French Canadians in Maillardville or the Vancouver Chinese. Well, here's a Chinese recipe that's popular in southern British Columbia (and among leg aficionados from other cultural backgrounds as well).

Green frog legs 1 pound
Dry sherry ½ tablespoon
Soy sauce 1 tablespoon
Cornstarch 2 tablespoons
Vegetable oil 1 cup, plus 1 tablespoon
Large bell pepper 1, cut into 1-inch squares
Garlic 1 tablespoon minced
Hot bean paste 1 tablespoon
Chinese red vinegar or red wine vinegar 1 tablespoon
Sugar ½ teaspoon
Sesame oil 1 teaspoon

1. Rinse frog legs and dry with paper towels. Split each pair apart and chop off feet. Halve legs crosswise through the joint.
2. In a bowl, mix frog legs with wine, soy sauce, and cornstarch.
3. Heat 1 cup oil in wok to 325°, drop in frog legs, and fry for 2 minutes. Remove frog legs with a slotted spoon and drain.
4. Empty all but 1 tablespoon oil from wok, add green pepper squares, and stir-fry for 1 minute over high heat. Remove to a plate.
5. Heat another tablespoon of the oil in wok, stir in garlic, and cook for 15 seconds; then blend in hot bean paste and cook for 10 more seconds. Add frog legs, green pepper, vinegar, sugar, and sesame oil, and mix thoroughly.
6. Transfer to a platter and serve immediately.

Serves 4

Sea Urchin Sauce for Lingcod or Rockfish

Sinclair Philip of Sooke Harbour House has discovered that the fruitiness of fresh sea urchin roe goes very well with white-fleshed fish and enhances their flavor. Accompany this dish with a delicate northwest gewürztraminer.

Whipping cream   ½ cup
Gewürztraminer*   2 tablespoons
Sea urchin roe   ½ cup chopped

1. In a small pan, bring cream and wine to a boil; reduce for 2 to 3 minutes.
2. Add roe and stir well to give the sauce a pretty orange color. Serve hot.

* A good British Columbia or Washington State gewürztraminer may be the best wine for this sauce (Alsatian traminers overpower the roe). Dry pear cider may be used instead of wine, but the quantity must be reduced to 1 tablespoon or the sea urchin roe will be overpowered by the cider.

Makes about 1 cup, enough for 2 servings

Sooke Harbour House Chive and Watercress Sauce

This sauce is good for such mild-tasting fish as sole, sand dabs, cod, or rockfish.

White wine   ¼ cup
Shallots   1 tablespoon finely chopped
Fish stock (see Index)   4 cups
Whipping cream   ¾ cup
Cold water   1 tablespoon
Chives   ½ cup chopped
Watercress   ⅓ cup chopped
Unsalted butter (see Index)   1 teaspoon, softened
Lemon juice   3 tablespoons

1. In small pan reduce wine and shallots over high heat until shallots are tender and wine has almost evaporated. Set aside.
2. In a 1-gallon pan, bring stock and whipping cream to a boil and reduce liquids until a creamy consistency is reached. Set aside.
3. In a blender, place water, chives, watercress, and butter and process. Add shallot/wine mixture and fish stock/cream mixture and process well. Stir in lemon juice and serve.

Makes 5 cups

Giant Pacific Horse Mussel Sauce for Pacific Cod

Here's a good recipe for the giant Pacific horse mussel that makes excellent use of this coarser relative of the delicate blue mussel. This rich, orange-colored sauce complements such bland fishes as the inexpensive Pacific cod very well.

Very dry white wine or vermouth   ¼ cup
Shallot   1, finely minced
Fish stock (see Index)   ½ cup
Whipping cream   ½ cup
Mussel meat*   ½ cup finely chopped
Chervil or dill   ½ cup minced

1. In medium saucepan, bring wine and shallot to boil. Reduce heat and cook until wine/shallot mixture reaches a syrupy consistency. Add stock and cream and let mixture cook until it thickens (up to 10 minutes). When sauce is finished, pour into blender with majority of chopped mussel meat and chervil; blend well. Add remaining mussels. Stir well to blend. (The sauce may be prepared up to this point earlier in the day.)
2. When fish is near serving point, reheat mussel sauce on a gentle flame. Correct seasoning to taste and serve with fish.

* The mussels for this dish are steamed open, have their beards (byssus threads) removed, and are then finely minced. A few larger chunks should be kept to improve the texture of the sauce. Other orange-fleshed mussels may be substituted.

Serves 2

Shrimp and Snow Peas

This is a perfect early summer luncheon dish. Accompany it with a dry northwest white wine.

Garlic clove   1, crushed in skin
Vegetable oil   2 tablespoons
Celery stalks   2 cups thinly sliced on the bias
Gingerroot   ½ teaspoon finely grated
Snow or sugar snap peas   2 cups
Meadow mushrooms, shiitake mushrooms, or commercial mushrooms   1½ cups sliced
Cold water   ⅓ cup
Light soy sauce   1 tablespoon
Dry sherry or mirin   1 tablespoon
Lemon juice   1 tablespoon
Cornstarch   2 teaspoons
Tiny fresh pink shrimp   2½ cups
Salt   to taste
Rice

1. Heat garlic in oil in heavy iron skillet or wok 1 minute, then discard. Add celery, ginger, and peas; cook and stir 2 minutes. Add mushrooms; cook and stir 1 minute.
2. Combine water, soy sauce, sherry, lemon juice, and cornstarch; add with shrimp to vegetables. Cook and stir until sauce bubbles and thickens. Season with salt to taste. Serve over hot rice.

Serves 4

Freshly Cooked Shrimp in Herb Dressing

The kinds and quantities of herbs used in this recipe are quite flexible; you may use fresh dill, tarragon, chervil, lovage, parsley, basil, or whatever else is fresh in your garden. Just remember, the taste of the dish will change with different herbs. Serve with a well-chilled dry chardonnay or sparkling wine.

Tarragon vinegar   2 tablespoons
Imported mustard   ¼ teaspoon
Salt and freshly ground black pepper   to taste
Vegetable oil   6 tablespoons
Nasturtium buds   1 tablespoon finely chopped
Parsley   2 tablespoons finely chopped
Tarragon   2 tablespoons chopped
Shrimp   1½ pounds, cooked in the shell and shelled
Lemon juice   from ½ lemon
Boston lettuce leaves   8
Quail eggs   8, hard-cooked, divided lengthwise
Salmon caviar   4 teaspoons drained
Edible borage flowers   4

1. Blend vinegar, mustard, salt, and pepper. Slowly dribble in oil as you beat mixture with wire whisk. Blend well.
2. Add nasturtium buds, parsley, and tarragon. Blend well.
3. Place shrimp in bowl; squeeze lemon juice over it. Add herb sauce and blend well. Do not crush shrimp.
4. Arrange 2 lettuce leaves on each of 4 platters. Spoon equal portions of shrimp onto lettuce. Garnish each with 4 quail egg halves (sunny side up) at the margins and with ¼ teaspoon of salmon caviar in center. Place a blue borage flower in center of each mound of caviar.

Serves 4

Shrimp in Beer

This is a nice luncheon dish and a great dish for a beach party—to be enjoyed shortly after you have pulled up your shrimp pots and harvested the wiggly bounty. Accompany this dish with a good lager beer and serve with melted butter, lemon, and home-baked bread.

Shrimp   5 to 6 pounds unpeeled
Beer   to cover
Salt water   1 cup
Bay leaf or juniper berries   1 (or to taste)
Garlic cloves   6, lightly crushed
Black peppercorns   12
Gingerroot   1 piece the size of a hazelnut, crushed

1. If shrimp are still alive, quickly immerse in boiling water to kill. Remove as soon as they turn red.
2. Combine other ingredients; bring to a boil. Add shrimp; cook 5 minutes. Turn off heat and let shrimp stay in beer 5 more minutes.

Serves 4 to 6

Whiskey-Baked Crab Meat

There always seems to be a lot of leftover crab meat every time we have a crab feast. Here's a tasty way of using it up.

Dungeness or rock crab meat   2 pounds cooked
Unsalted butter (see Index)   ½ cup, melted
Nuoc mam   ¼ teaspoon
Freshly ground white pepper   to taste
Lemon juice   from 1 lemon
Parsley or chervil   1 tablespoon finely chopped
Whiskey (preferably Skagit moonshine)   4 tablespoons

Place crab meat in shallow baking dish. Pour melted butter over crab. Season with nuoc mam and pepper. Squeeze lemon juice over crab. Sprinkle with parsley and whiskey. Bake at 375° until hot (for about 10 minutes).

Serves 4 to 6

Rock Crab with Ginger Butter Sauce

This is a very good recipe for freshly cooked crab as well as for leftovers from a previous day's crab feast. Do not use frozen crab. Accompany this dish with a well-chilled gewürztraminer or premium lager beer and freshly baked french bread.

Rock crab   4, cooked
Unsalted butter (see Index)   ¼ cup
Green onion   ¼ cup, white and green portions, thinly sliced on the bias
Gingerroot   1 teaspoon finely grated
Dry sauvignon blanc   ¼ cup

1. Clean crab under cold running water. Reserve crab "butter" inside shell. (Crab butter is the soft, butterlike substance found inside the crab's carapace.) Break each crab into 2 to 4 pieces (depending on size of crab). Gently crack legs.
2. Steam crab on rack over hot water for 5 minutes or until heated through. Melt butter in heavy skillet; stir in onion and gingerroot. Carefully, over low heat, blend in crab "butter." Cook gently for 5 minutes. Stir wine into butter mixture. Cook and stir gently until reduced and thickened. Serve as a dipping sauce with crab.

Serves 4

Crab-Fried Rice

This is a nice luncheon dish. Whole pea crabs or tiny beach crabs may be substituted for the crab meat. The pea crabs can be eaten whole, shell and all; the beach crabs must be cracked and shelled. If fresh geoduck is unavailable, Manila or littleneck clams may be used instead, though the dish will not have the same quality.

Vegetable oil   3 tablespoons
Garlic cloves   2, finely chopped
Shallots   3, finely chopped
Green onion   1 tablespoon finely sliced
Chives   1 tablespoon finely sliced
Geoduck belly meat   2 cups cut into ¼-inch cubes
Cooked crab meat   ½ cup
Peas   1 cup
Brown rice   3 cups cooked (or 1½ cups rice, 1½ cups wheat berries)
Light soy sauce   1 teaspoon
Nuoc mam   ¼ teaspoon

1. Heat pan and add oil. When oil is hot, add garlic, shallots, green onion, and chives. Sauté until chives wilt.
2. Add geoduck, crab, and peas; sauté for 5 minutes. Add rice. Cook over medium heat until rice is heated through (10 to 30 minutes), stirring regularly to mix ingredients and to keep rice and seafood from sticking to pan. Season with soy sauce and nuoc mam when rice has finished cooking. Serve hot.

Serves 4 to 6

Crab Crêpes

You must pick the tart red huckleberries called for in this recipe yourself, but the dish is well worth the effort. This sauce is also good served over mild white fish. Accompany the crêpes with a dry, fruity riesling or gewürztraminer.

Unsalted butter (see Index)   3 tablespoons
Flour   3 tablespoons
Sauvignon blanc   1 cup
Salt and freshly ground white pepper   to taste
Crème fraîche (see Index)   ½ cup
Dungeness or rock crab meat   1 pound
Crêpe batter*   enough for 6
Red Huckleberry-Hazelnut Sauce
Unsalted butter (see Index)   ½ cup, melted

1. In saucepan, make roux by melting butter, blending in flour, and cooking for 2 minutes over low heat. Gradually add wine, stirring constantly, until mixture bubbles and thickens. Season with salt and pepper; blend in crème fraîche, stirring until smooth. Gently fold in crab meat. Keep warm over very low heat, stirring occasionally.
2. Make crêpes.
3. Preheat oven to 375°. Place about ⅓ cup crab filling on center of each crêpe. Pour a stripe of Red Huckleberry-Hazelnut Sauce on top of crab meat. Roll crêpe and place seam side down in baking dish. Repeat until all crêpes are filled. Brush with melted butter.
5. Bake on top shelf of oven for 15 minutes or until hot and bubbly.
6. Serve with remaining sauce.

* Use any standard crêpe recipe.

Serves 4 to 6

Red Huckleberry-Hazelnut Sauce

Unsalted butter (see Index)   4 tablespoons
Red huckleberries   1 cup
Hazelnuts   2 tablespoons finely chopped
Shallot   1 tablespoon finely chopped
Lemon juice   1 tablespoon

Melt butter in heavy skillet. Add other ingredients and cook over medium heat until huckleberries are soft. Mash with fork. Reduce heat and cook sauce down until quite thick.

Makes about 1 cup

Sautéed Scallops

Make sure to buy only fresh scallops with closed shells. If the shell is open the scallop will be dead—scallops dry out and die very quickly. Cook scallops as soon as you get them to your kitchen (or shuck them right away and cook them later). If scallops contain roe, use it for garnishing; otherwise use fish roe. Accompany this dish with a dry sauvignon blanc.

Unsalted butter (see Index)   6 tablespoons
Whole pink scallops   48
Salt and freshly ground white pepper   to taste
Parlsey   4 tablespoons finely chopped
Gingerroot   4 thin slices, peeled
Salmon caviar, steelhead caviar, or golden whitefish caviar   2 to 3 teaspoons
Lemon wedges   garnish

1. Melt butter in skillet. When hot and foamy, add scallops; cover. Cook over medium heat until scallops open, about 3 to 5 minutes.
2. Remove scallops from pan and reserve scallop juices. Add salt, pepper, parsley, ginger, and scallop nectar. Stir well and cook for a few minutes more. Discard ginger.
3. Arrange scallops on individual serving dishes. Remove top shell from each scallop. Spoon a little of the butter sauce over each scallop. Garnish each with a few salmon caviar eggs or ½ teaspoon steelhead or whitefish caviar. Serve with lemon wedges on the side.

Serves 4 to 6

Vancouver Honey Scallops

Curry has been popular in the Pacific Northwest ever since the British settled here.

Sea scallops, muscle only   2 pounds
Honey   ¼ cup
Curry powder   1 teaspoon
Prepared mustard   ¼ cup
Lemon juice   1 teaspoon

1. Line broiler pan with aluminum foil and arrange scallops in bottom of pan.
2. Combine remaining ingredients and mix well.
3. Brush scallops generously with curry mixture.
4. Place broiler pan in lowest position under source of heat and broil scallops for 10 minutes.
5. Turn scallops, brush with curry mixture, and broil 10 minutes longer or until nicely browned.

Serves 4

Pacific Rock Scallops with Champagne Roe Sauce

Many seafood connoisseurs consider the Pacific rock scallop (Hinnites giganteus) to be our tastiest shellfish. In the 19th century a thriving industry was built around this delectable mollusc. Unfortunately rock scallops, like other toothsome marine creatures, have suffered from overharvesting. They are not as common as they used to be, but are well worth seeking out. Rockfish roe is also very tasty. The following recipe comes from Sinclair Philip of Sooke Harbour House.

Pacific rock scallops*　6
Champagne　½ cup, room temperature
Whipping cream　½ cup
Rock scallop shells (to be heated in oven)　6
Unsalted butter (see Index)　2 tablespoons
Edible borage flowers　garnish

1. Shuck rock scallops; save the prettier shells where purple or mauve colors are prominent. Remove roe and white scallop muscle. Discard viscera (unless you are sure there is no red tide). Cut muscle in half horizontally.
2. Cut roe into small pieces with sharp knife. Do not mash. Set aside.
3. Bring champagne to a boil; then reduce by half. Add whipping cream and reduce by half again. Finish sauce by incorporating roe and cooking for 20 seconds.
4. Sauté halved scallop muscles in butter for about 30 seconds on each side over high heat.
5. Arrange scallop muscles on preheated shells. Pour sauce over. Garnish with borage flowers.

* Both the roe and the meat are excellent for only a few hours after you collect this tasty mollusc. But, if you keep them longer, cook both. (Remember: you've got to collect your own; it's not legal to collect rock scallops commercially.)

Serves 2

Crawfish in Apple Cider

This recipe calls for a dry cider made from tart apples. You may have trouble using the sweet ciders sold in our stores—unless you have a sweet tooth—but you should have no difficulty finding a nice, tart cider at a roadside stand or at a farmers' market. Serve with mashed potatoes, crisp-cooked vegetables, and a chilled dry sauvignon blanc or semillon or, if you have used sweet cider, with a sweet riesling.

Cooked, peeled crawfish tails　1½ pounds, preferably same size
Unsalted butter (see Index)　3 tablespoons
Shallots　2 tablespoons finely chopped
Concentrated dry cider*　2 tablespoons
Heavy cream　¾ cup
Salt and freshly ground black pepper　to taste

1. Rinse crawfish tails under cold running water, remove vein running down the back, and pat dry.
2. Melt butter in a heavy skillet and add tails and shallots.
3. Add concentrated cider and stir.
4. Remove tails with slotted spoon. Keep warm.
5. Add cream to skillet and cook over high heat for 1 minute. Add salt and pepper to taste. Return crawfish tails to skillet and cook just to heat through.

* Boil down 1 cup of dry cider until you have 2 tablespoons of concentrate. If you like a stronger flavor, boil down 2 cups.

Serves 4 to 6

Abalone Sooke Harbour House

This recipe calls for fresh abalone, a treat that can be enjoyed along our entire coastline (even though these tasty snails are not exactly plentiful).

Medium-sized abalone   2
Unsalted butter (see Index)   2 tablespoons
Garlic   ¼ tablespoon minced
Shallot   ¼ tablespoon minced
Celery   2-inch piece, finely julienned
Leek   3-inch piece, finely julienned
Carrot   2-inch piece, finely julienned
Nuoc mam   4 drops
Lemon thyme   ½ teaspoon minced
Fennel seed   ½ teaspoon
Hazelnuts   2 tablespoons sliced
Fish stock (see Index)   ½ cup
Lemon   ¼

1. Wrap fresh abalone in plastic and place in freezer until quite firm. (The freezing relaxes the muscle, making it easier to handle.) To remove shell, lift up muscle and separate it from shell with a sharp knife. Rinse shell clean and set aside for decoration. Scrub off black coating on muscle and cut muscle in half horizontally; then cut into very thin strips.
2. Melt butter in medium-sized skillet over medium heat. Add next 9 ingredients and sauté for 1 minute. Add stock; stir well. Add abalone. Bring heat to high; distribute abalone evenly in pan.
3. Cook for maximum of 1 minute, stirring constantly. (Overcooking will toughen the abalone.) Squeeze juice from lemon over abalone. Place abalone shells on warm serving plates and arrange cooked abalone in shells.

Serves 2

Baked Oysters in Cream

I like my oysters raw, but if you prefer eating these delicate molluscs cooked, here's a delectable way of preparing them. Accompany this dish with a dry white or sparkling wine.

Medium oysters on the half shell   24
Heavy cream   1¼ cups
Goat cheese or white Cheddar cheese   ¾ cup grated
Freshly ground white pepper   to taste
Unsalted butter (see Index)   ½ cup, melted
Rock salt to hold oysters in baking dish   as needed

1. Place oysters open-faced in a baking dish on a bed of rock salt. Pour cream over oysters, making sure not to spill any onto salt. (I like to thicken the cream for this dish by letting it sit outside the refrigerator for a day; then I freeze it for a day, let it thaw, and scoop the thick part off the top.)
2. Sprinkle oysters with grated cheese and pepper. Carefully dribble butter over cheese. Place dish in oven and broil 5 minutes (do not let them burn), 2 inches from heating unit, or bake in 400° oven for 7 to 10 minutes.

Serves 4 to 6 as a luncheon dish; 2 to 4 as a dinner course

Oysters Baked in Shells

Small oysters are best eaten on the half shell, but sometimes you get stuck with some that are just too large to swallow raw. Here's one way to fix them properly. Accompany these oysters with a fruity Château Benoit brut.

Large oysters   24, shucked, lower shells reserved
Egg   1
Salt and freshly ground white pepper   to taste
Parsley   1 tablespoon finely chopped
Cold water   1 tablespoon
Fine bread or cracker crumbs   1 cup
Unsalted butter (see Index)   4 to 6 tablespoons
Rock salt to hold oysters in baking dish   as needed

1. Scrub oyster shells carefully to remove any seaweed or dirt. (Shells may be soaked and preheated by immersion in hot water.)
2. Beat egg while seasoning and adding water.
3. Dip oysters into egg mixture, then into crumbs.
4. Return oysters to shells; dot with butter, and bake in 450° oven for 10 minutes.

Serves 4

Potato Clam Cakes

This is a beach cabin lunch or dinner and should be accompanied with a hearty northwest ale or stout, or with a good white jug wine.

Geoduck or horse clam siphon   2 cups ground
Medium onion   1, grated
Raw potatoes   2 cups finely grated
Large eggs   2, lightly beaten
Paprika   pinch
Parsley or chervil   1 teaspoon finely chopped
Salt and freshly ground black pepper   to taste
Flour   as needed
Bacon drippings   as needed

1. Mix all ingredients except bacon drippings, using just enough flour to hold mixture together.
2. Fry like hot cakes in ¼-inch-deep hot bacon drippings until brown on both sides.
3. Drain on layer of paper towels; serve hot.

Serves 2 to 4

Squid in Ink

The idea of serving squid in its own ink does not appeal to some people, but it is really quite delicious. Just make sure the squid used in this dish has never been frozen. It's best to jig for your own squid from a pier, take your catch home, and cook it immediately.

Squid   2 pounds, cleaned, ink sac reserved
Medium onions   2, chopped
Garlic clove   1, crushed
Unsalted butter (see Index)   ½ cup, clarified
Salt   ¼ teaspoon
Cayenne   pinch
Cold water   ½ cup

1. Slit open the squids' bodies and flatten. Cut into 1-inch-square pieces. Set aside on paper towels to dry.
2. Gently sauté onion and garlic in butter until onions are translucent. Add squid, salt, and cayenne.
3. Break ink sac and pour ink into pan; stir to blend. Add water, cover, and simmer gently for 2 hours. (Be sure to check the squid at regular intervals to make sure the liquids haven't cooked away. Add more water if necessary.)

Serves 4 to 6

Shredded Pheasant Salad

This is a Chinese recipe, originally made with chicken. But I like it much better with farm-raised pheasant (and I have even enjoyed wild duck prepared this way). Matching a wine to a Chinese dish can be an exercise in frustration, but I have enjoyed an off-dry sauvignon blanc with this one. You might, however, just settle for a good lager beer or light ale.

Whole pheasant breasts with skin   2
Vegetable oil   for deep-frying
Won ton squares   8, cut into ⅛-inch strips
Rice noodles   2 ounces
Light soy sauce   ¼ cup
Prepared Chinese mustard   1 tablespoon
Dark Chinese sesame oil   1 teaspoon
Five spice powder   1 teaspoon
Prepared Jellyfish   ½ cup shredded
Green onion   ½ cup sliced
Hazelnuts   ¼ cup chopped and toasted
Chinese cabbage   1 head, shredded

1. Cook pheasant breasts, covered, in boiling salted water for 20 minutes, or until tender. Drain well; dry with paper towels. Remove skin. Place breasts 1 at a time in hot (365°) oil for 3 to 4 minutes, until crisp and golden (use heavy wok or cast-iron frying pan to heat oil). Drain on paper towels. Remove meat from bone; tear into shreds or cut into very fine strips.
2. In same oil, fry won ton strips, a quarter at a time, until golden, about 30 seconds. Then fry rice noodles, also a quarter at a time. Remove rice noodles as soon as they puff up so that they do not become grease-soaked. Drain well.
3. In large bowl, combine soy sauce, mustard, sesame oil, and spice powder. Add pheasant, jellyfish, and onion; toss to coat well. Cover and chill. Just before serving, add rice noodles, won ton strips, and hazelnuts. Toss gently. To serve, pile salad onto bed of shredded Chinese cabbage.

Serves 4

Prepared Jellyfish

Dried jellyfish is available in oriental food markets throughout the Pacific Northwest. This somewhat unusual food, which is very popular among Asian immigrants, adds an interesting crunchy texture to salads. It is excellent in shredded pheasant salad, but may be added to other salads as well. It has little taste of its own and takes on the taste of the sauce in which it is marinated.

Dried shredded jellyfish   6 ounces
Light soy sauce   1 tablespoon
Rice or white wine vinegar   1 tablespoon
Sugar   ¼ teaspoon
Chinese sesame oil   ¼ teaspoon
Chinese oyster sauce   1 teaspoon
Cayenne   pinch

1. Wash dried jellyfish thoroughly with cold water to remove salt. Place jellyfish in a large bowl and cover with cold water. Soak for 48 hours or longer to leach out remaining salt. Change water every 6 to 12 hours.
2. Drain jellyfish. Place strips in a strainer; pour 1 cup of very hot (160° to 180°) water over it; rinse immediately with cold water and drain.
3. In small bowl, mix soy sauce, vinegar, sugar, sesame oil, oyster sauce, and cayenne. Combine jellyfish with sauce and chill for 2 hours.
4. If served in a salad, drain well before adding. If served by itself as an appetizer, mix with ½ cup finely julienned Japanese cucumber (for contrasting texture) just before serving.

Serves 4; makes 1½ to 2 cups

Hazelnut Chicken with Meadow Mushrooms

This dish is best when newly emerged buttons of meadow mushrooms are used. If you cannot find meadow mushrooms, use cultivated oyster mushrooms, or tops and top inch of enokitake mushrooms (as a last resort, you may use very fresh *commercial mushrooms.) This goes very well with a dry northwest sauvignon blanc.*

Hazelnuts   ¼ cup quartered
Vegetable oil   6 tablespoons
Cornstarch   4 teaspoons
Water   2 teaspoons
Dry sherry   1 tablespoon
Chinese oyster sauce   1 tablespoon
Chicken breast   1 pound, boned and cubed
Dry sauvignon blanc   2 teaspoons
Egg white   ½
Freshly ground black pepper   to taste
Snow pea pods   ¼ pound
Water chestnuts*   ¼ cup
Heart of cattail stalk   ¼ cup, thinly sliced
Meadow mushroom buttons   24

1. Fry hazelnuts in 1 tablespoon oil until golden. Drain and set aside.
2. Blend 1 teaspoon cornstarch with 1 teaspoon water. Mix well and add sherry, oyster sauce, and 1 teaspoon water. Mix well and set aside.
3. Mix chicken, white wine, egg white, and 1 tablespoon cornstarch. Season to taste with pepper.
4. Heat 5 tablespoons oil in wok or heavy iron skillet. Add chicken and stir-fry until chicken is no longer pink. Add pea pods, water chestnuts, cattail heart, and mushrooms. Stir-fry for 3 minutes longer.
5. Stir sherry mixture and add to wok. Cook, stirring, 1 minute longer. Turn out onto serving platter and top with fried hazelnuts.

* At the risk of overrepeating, I have to say again that *fresh* water chestnuts are essential here.

Serves 4

Chicken with Garlic Nut Sauce

This recipe was adapted from a potato recipe in Constance Bollen's and Marlene Blessing's One Potato, Two Potato *cookbook. I thought the sauce sounded intriguing and would work well with chicken. It did.*

Unsalted butter (see Index)   2 tablespoons
Chicken breasts   2 (about 1½ pounds), skinned, boned, and halved
Garlic Nut Sauce

1. Heat butter in skillet until quite hot. When hot, but not brown, add chicken breasts. Cook pieces on one side over moderately high heat about 4 minutes. Turn and cook on the other side until golden brown, about 2 to 4 minutes. Cover and cook about 4 to 5 minutes or until tender.
2. Remove chicken from pan to heated serving platter. Spoon sauce over chicken. Serve hot.

Serves 4

Garlic Nut Sauce

Egg yolks   2
White wine vinegar   2 tablespoons
Lemon juice   1 tablespoon
Garlic cloves   4, peeled
Salt   ½ teaspoon
Olive oil   1 cup
Hazelnuts   ½ cup chopped and lightly toasted

1. In blender or food processor, combine egg yolks, vinegar, lemon juice, garlic, and salt. Process.
2. With machine at low speed, gradually add olive oil in a fine, steady stream, blending until a creamy consistency is achieved.
3. Add nuts and process until sauce is blended and thickened.

Makes 1½ to 1⅔ cups

Chicken with Mustard Sauce

This recipe comes from Mendy McLean-Stone of Coupeville. Mendy and her husband John frequently have out-of-town friends drop in unexpectedly—this is one of her favorite recipes for feeding them. The dish virtually bakes itself, while John and Mendy and their guests enjoy a first course of tender Penn Cove mussels. We have enjoyed this dish with a number of wines; a dry, very crisp Oregon chardonnay works best. Or try a dry northwest sauvignon blanc.

Chicken   5 pounds (approximately), cut-up
Unsalted butter (see Index)   6 to 8 tablespoons
Flour   as needed
Brandy   ¼ cup
Small mushrooms   1 pound (quarter mushrooms if using large ones)
Parsley   ¼ cup minced
Green onions or shallots   ¼ cup minced
Whipping cream   2 cups
Dijon-style mustard   2 tablespoons
Lemon juice   from ½ lemon
Egg yolks   3

1. Skin chicken if you want a less rich dish.
2. Melt 3 tablespoons butter in large heavy frying pan.
3. Dust skinned chicken with flour. Cook chicken over medium heat until golden brown on all sides, a few pieces at a time. Remove from pan when done and keep warm. When all pieces have been browned, return to pan and douse with warm brandy. Ignite brandy. Shake pan until flame dies. Remove chicken from pan and place in deep 3½- to 4-quart casserole. Pour pan juices over chicken.
4. Wipe pan clean. Melt remaining 3 tablespoons butter in pan. Sauté mushrooms, parsley, and onions until onions are soft but not brown. Slowly blend in cream, mustard, and lemon. Blend, bring to a boil, and pour over chicken. (Dish may be prepared ahead of time to this point and refrigerated overnight.)
5. Bake chicken in 375° oven for 55 minutes to 1 hour (1 hour if refrigerated).
6. Drain sauce from pan and place in large frying pan. Heat. Beat egg yolks. Add some of heated sauce to yolks, blend, and stir mixture into sauce. Blend well. Cook slowly over low heat until sauce thickens. Do not boil.
7. Pour a little of sauce over chicken. Serve remaining sauce in sauceboat so guests can help themselves. Serve hot.

Serves 6 to 8

Chicken Sautéed in Northwest Riesling

This recipe poses an interesting question: should one use a dry or a sweet riesling? Both appear to work well, though with somewhat different taste effects. (If you're going to try the recipe with a sweet riesling, you might want to add one teaspoon of white wine vinegar in addition to the wine.) Accompany with more of the same wine used for cooking the chicken.

Broiler chicken   2½ to 3 pounds, cut into 1-inch pieces
Salt and freshly ground black pepper   to taste
Unsalted butter (see Index)   2 tablespoons
Onion   ½ cup chopped
Medium garlic gloves   2, minced
Bay leaf   1
Whole cloves   2
Northwest riesling   1½ cups
Whipping cream   1 cup
Flour   2 tablespoons
Egg yolks   3, beaten
Nutmeg   to taste
Salt and freshly ground black pepper   to taste
Pasta

1. Sprinkle chicken pieces with salt and pepper. In large, heavy (12-inch) skillet, slowly brown chicken in butter (about 5 minutes). Add onion, garlic, bay leaf, cloves, and wine. Bring to boil; reduce heat. Cover and simmer till chicken is tender, about 20 to 30 minutes.
2. Remove chicken pieces to platter; keep warm. Discard bay leaf and cloves. Skim excess fat from pan juices. Quickly boil down pan juices and onion, uncovered, until reduced to 1¼ cups. Strain juices and set aside; discard onion.
3. Shake together whipping cream and flour in a jar. In saucepan, beat together whipping cream mixture, egg yolks, and seasonings. Cook and stir until thickened, but do not boil. Serve chicken and sauce over hot noodles.

Serves 4

Chicken Val d'Aostano

The Osteria Mitchelli is a Seattle restaurant that specializes in northwest food with an Italian twist. In this chicken dish, which is best when made with Oregon or Washington chickens, I have successfully substituted local country ham for the prosciutto and Pleasant Valley Gouda for the fontina. Accompany this dish with a fruity sauvignon blanc or semillon.

Chicken breasts   4 halves, skinned and boned
Prosciutto   4 slices
Fontina cheese   4 ounces
Flour
Unsalted butter (see Index)   ½ cup
Garlic cloves   4, minced
Rosemary   1 tablespoon crushed
Dry white wine   1 cup

1. Cut a pocket into each breast half; line pocket with ham slice. Place 1 ounce cheese in each pocket.
2. Flour breasts, sauté in melted butter for 2 minutes on each side. Add garlic, rosemary, and white wine. Cover pan. Cook 10 minutes. Add water if pan dries out.

Serves 4

Chicken with Tomatoes and Zucchini

This simple but delectable dish was served to us by Mendy McLean-Stone of Coupeville. Mendy and her husband John are part-owners of the historic Captain Whidbey Inn (the place that's known for its restless ghost). Make sure to use only garden-fresh vegetables for this dish (both tomatoes and zucchini ripen very well on Whidbey Island, which is located right in the middle of Puget Sound's so-called "banana belt").

Chicken legs and thighs   6 pieces
Flour   as needed
Unsalted butter (see Index)   4 to 6 tablespoons
Dill   ¼ teaspoon
Oregano   ¼ teaspoon
Tomatoes   2 to 3, cubed
Medium zucchini   2 to 3, cubed
Salt and freshly ground black pepper   to taste

Dredge chicken in flour. Brown in butter in heavy skillet. Sprinkle dill and oregano over chicken. Add tomato and zucchini. Season with salt and pepper. Bake in 350° oven, covered, for 30 to 40 minutes. Serve hot.

Serves 4

Sautéed Chicken Breasts with Apple Dill Sauce

Use only tender, flavorful northwest chicken for this dish. Our chicken, which is raised on barley, wheat, and other hard grains, has a whiter meat and better taste than the greasy, yellow-fatted chicken that comes to us from the southern states. The latter may be good for gumbo or enchiladas, but does not lend itself to delicate dishes the way northwest-raised chicken does. Accompany this dish with rice, steamed vegetables, and a dry riesling or sauvignon blanc.

Unsalted butter (see Index)   5 tablespoons
Chicken breasts   4, skinned
Cornstarch   1 tablespoon
Honey   1 tablespoon
Dijon-style mustard   ½ teaspoon
Dill   1 teaspoon or
    Dried dill   ½ teaspoon
Applejack or Calvados   ½ cup
Cooking apple   ½ cup unpeeled and diced
Lemon peel and lemon juice   from 1 lemon
Nuoc mam   ½ teaspoon

1. Melt 4 tablespoons butter in heavy skillet. When hot, add chicken breasts, a couple at a time, and sauté 3 to 5 minutes on each side. Arrange on individual plates; keep warm.
2. In the meantime, in a separate pan, melt 1 tablespoon butter. Remove from heat; stir in cornstarch, honey, mustard, and dill. Gradually blend in applejack. Add diced apple, lemon peel, and lemon juice. Season with nuoc mam. Cook over medium heat, stirring constantly until thickened. Immediately pour over chicken breasts; serve hot.

Serves 4

Sharon Anderson's Spit-Roasted Chicken

Sharon runs one of the nicest little art galleries in the Northwest, the La Conner Gallery located in an old building on La Conner's waterfront. She's also an excellent cook. Here's one of her favorites. It takes a bit of preparing, but it's well worth it. Serve with a light riesling or chenin blanc.

Whole large chicken   1
Garlic cloves   2, peeled
Sage leaves   4 to 5
Large parsley sprigs   2 to 3
Medium onion   ½, coarsely chopped or
    Green onions   2 to 3 coarsely chopped
Celery stems with tops   2 or 3
Olive oil   as needed
Lemon juice   from ½ lemon
Golden Rice Casserole

1. Stuff chicken with garlic, sage, parsley, onion, and celery.
2. Rub outside of chicken with olive oil and lemon juice.
3. Tuck extra sprigs of parsley and sage between chicken's legs and wings.
4. Truss chicken and place on spit. Slowly roast on turning spit over white barbecue coals or electric rotisserie for about 2 hours, until golden and fragrant. Serve with Golden Rice Casserole.

Serves 2 to 4

Golden Rice Casserole

White rice   1 cup
Shortening   3 tablespoons
Onion   ½ cup chopped
Salt   ¾ teaspoon
Freshly ground black pepper   ⅛ teaspoon
Flour   1 tablespoon
Milk   ¾ cup
Cheddar cheese   1½ cups shredded

1. Cook rice according to package directions.
2. Sauté onion in shortening until browned; add salt, pepper, flour, blend.
3. Add milk, stir, and cook until thickened. Remove from heat, add cheese; stir until cheese has melted and sauce is well blended.
4. Add rice; blend.
5. Pour into greased casserole and bake in a 350° oven for 30 minutes. Serve hot.

Serves 2 to 4

"Stormy" Turkey

The notorious 1983 Thanksgiving Storm knocked down power lines throughout the Puget Sound region. Many a family, caught with a partially cooked turkey in the oven, rushed from friend's house to friend's house, trying to find an oven with a power supply and hoping to get their bird cooked before it cooled and spoiled. They need not have worried had they had access to simple "pioneer" appliances, a large dutch oven and a working fireplace. You may even add your yams, potatoes, et al. to the turkey in the dutch oven for that "complete" Thanksgiving meal.

Turkey   one, 8 to 10 pounds, disjointed
Flour   1 cup
Salt and freshly ground black pepper   to taste
Bacon grease   ¼ cup
Hot water   ½ cup

1. Dredge turkey parts in flour seasoned with salt and pepper and brown in bacon grease in large dutch oven.
2. Add a little hot water, put on lid, and cover lid with fireplace coals. Bank hot coals around sides of oven. Cook for 2 to 4 hours, depending on the size of your turkey, adding small amounts of hot water from time to time if neccessary.

Wild Drunken Duck

Fat rich wines like a Yakima Valley merlot or Kiona lemberger go well with wild duck, but so do sweetish rieslings and gewürztraminers. You thus have quite a bit of leeway when choosing the wine for cooking this duck; better yet, if you are a successful nimrod, try them all in turn.

Wild ducks   1 pair
Unsalted butter (see Index)   1 tablespoon
Sweet onions   2, chopped
Country ham   ¼ cup very finely minced
Turnips   6, cut in quarters or diced
Flour   1 tablespoon sifted
Bay leaves   2
Light soy sauce or salt   dash
Freshly ground black pepper   to taste
Merlot or lemberger wine   1 bottle

1. Clean ducks and cut into pieces at the joints.
2. Melt butter in heavy cast-iron pot; add onions. When onion has browned, add duck. After duck has browned, add ham, turnips, and flour. Stir well, let flour brown slightly, and add seasonings. Let simmer for 15 minutes, then add sufficient wine to cover ducks. Stir well, cover tightly, and let cook for another 30 minutes.

Serves 2 to 4

Spring Lamb Chops and Wild Mushrooms

I just love the flavor of Pacific Northwest lamb with its subtleness and complexity. Wild mushrooms, whether chanterelles, boletes, or morels, go very well with lamb and add to the enjoyment of this tasty meat. Try to combine the two as often as possible. Or use some of the interesting fresh mushrooms available commercially in our region—shiitake, oyster mushrooms, et al. Accompany this dish with a premium porter or stout.

Thin loin chops   6 (about 1½ pounds)
Unsalted butter (see Index)   2 tablespoons
Large Walla Walla onion   1, sliced
Wild mushrooms   ½ pound, sliced
Mild green Zillah chili pepper   1, peeled, seeded, and cut into thin strips
Lemon   6 thin slices
Freshly ground black pepper   to taste
Light soy sauce   ¼ cup
Dry sherry   ¼ cup
Lemon juice   from ½ lemon
Gingerroot   1 teaspoon
Garlic cloves   2, finely chopped

1. In heavy 12-inch skillet, brown chops on both sides in 1 tablespoon butter; remove from skillet. Set aside.
2. Add remaining tablespoon butter to skillet; sauté onion, mushrooms, and chili pepper. Remove from skillet. Set aside and keep warm.
3. Return chops to skillet; top with onion, mushrooms, pepper, and lemon slices. Combine remaining ingredients; pour over chops. Cover, cooking over medium heat 20 minutes or until chops are cooked to desired doneness.

Serves 4 to 6

Baked Lamb Chops in Cider Sauce

Northwest apple cider and northwest lamb match each other's taste beautifully. Accompany this dish with a good hard cider or even an applejack or apple brandy.

Shoulder lamb chops   6
Freshly ground black pepper   to taste
Oil   2 tablespoons
Light soy sauce or nuoc mam   1 teaspoon
Green onion   ¼ cup chopped
Cooking apples   2, peeled, seeded, and chopped
Cider vinegar   2 tablespoons
Basil   1 tablespoon chopped
Gingerroot   2 teaspoons grated
Dry apple cider   ¼ cup

1. Season chops with pepper. Place oil in large, heavy skillet. Brown chops in hot oil, 2 to 3 minutes on each side. Remove and place in 13- by 9- by 2-inch baking pan.
2. Combine remaining ingredients in skillet. Stir for 2 minutes to deglaze pan; then raise heat and reduce excess liquid to thicken sauce.
3. Pour sauce over chops. Bake in a 375° oven for 30 to 40 minutes or until chops are cooked to desired degree of doneness. Baste meat occasionally with pan juices to keep it moist. Serve hot with sauce (stir sauce to blend after removing meat; then pour).

Serves 6

Lamb Chops with Sesame Onion Sauce

My favorite lamb comes from the gravelly pastures of the San Juan and Gulf Islands, but the dry ridges east of the Cascades in British Columbia, Washington, and Oregon also grow superb lamb. Lemberger, a new red wine in the Northwest, seems to go particularly well with lamb, especially the rich lemberger made by Kiona in the Yakima Valley. Accompany this dish with rice and crisp-cooked vegetables.

Thick lamb chops   twelve, 2 inches thick, trimmed of most fat
Sweet Walla Walla onions   4 cups sliced
Garlic   1 tablespoon finely chopped
Olive oil   2 tablespoons
Soy sauce   2 tablespoons
Toasted white sesame seeds   2 tablespoons
White wine vinegar   1 tablespoon
Thyme   ½ teaspoon chopped
Rosemary   ½ teaspoon chopped
Freshly ground black pepper   to taste

1. Place each chop on a flat, hard surface and pound lightly with a mallet or the side of a Chinese cleaver. Place chops on a barbecue or hibachi grill; cook on each side for about 5 minutes.
2. In the meantime, sauté onions and garlic in oil 5 minutes, stirring frequently. Add remaining ingredients. Cook 5 minutes longer or until onions are tender-crisp.
3. Arrange chops on serving platter. Spoon sauce over chops. Serve hot.

Serves 6

Lamb and Oysters

Here's a dish that draws upon the products of land and sea. To do justice to both of the two main ingredients, I'd accompany this dish with a good northwest ale, stout, or porter, and with ample french bread for sopping up the juices.

Small lamb chops   eight, 1-inch-thick, trimmed of most fat
Large garlic cloves   2, mashed
Olive oil   2 tablespoons
Salt and freshly ground black pepper   to taste
Unsalted butter (see Index)   4 tablespoons
Pale ale   ¼ cup
Tiny Pacific yearling oysters   48, freshly shucked, liquor reserved
Chervil or parsley   2 tablespoons chopped

1. Rub each lamb chop with garlic. Brush with oil on both sides. Cook 3 to 4 minutes on each side in heavy iron skillet over medium-high heat. Season to taste with salt and pepper.
2. Remove from pan. Melt butter in pan. As soon as butter has melted, add ale. Boil vigorously to reduce by half. Add oysters and their liquor; sprinkle with chervil. Cook only until oysters curl at edges. Immediately remove from pan and spoon onto lamb chops, dividing everything equally.
3. Continue to boil and reduce sauce until it thickens. Spoon over lamb chops and oysters. Serve immediately.

Serves 4

Crown Roast of Lamb

Have your butcher put the crown together for you—but make sure he uses Pacific Northwest lamb. Lamb from other parts of the country and imported lamb is just not as tasty. Accompany this dish with a hearty red wine or with a premium stout, ale, or porter.

Chanterelle mushrooms   1 cup coarsely chopped
Unsalted butter (see Index)   2 tablespoons
Oysters   1 cup freshly shucked
Oyster liquor   2 tablespoons
Dry bread crumbs   1 cup
Celery   ½ cup chopped
Onion   2 tablespoons finely chopped
Unsalted butter (see Index)   4 tablespoons
Salt and freshly ground black pepper   to taste
Bacon slices   as needed (1 for each rib end of the roast, plus a few extra slices)
Lamb crown, assembled   1

1. Sauté mushrooms in butter until soft. Chop oysters coarsely; add to pan. Sauté for 2 minutes. Add other ingredients except lamb and bacon. Blend in; then stuff crown. Wrap bacon around rib ends to prevent charring and arrange a few slices of bacon across stuffing.
2. Roast in a moderate oven (350°) 30 to 35 minutes per pound. When roast is done, remove bacon from rib ends and replace with paper frills.

Allow 2 ribs for each serving

Marinated Lamb

This dish is a rather extensive modification of a popular dish served at Ray's Boathouse in Seattle. It calls for the best of northwest lamb and wine. I enjoy it with a Yakima Valley merlot, but a first-rate cabernet sauvignon will also work well.

Yakima Valley merlot   2 cups
Nuoc mam   1 tablespoon
Oregano   2 tablespoons chopped
Thyme   2 tablespoons chopped
Freshly ground coarse black pepper   2 teaspoons
Onion   ¼ cup chopped
Garlic cloves   12, minced
Parsley   ¼ cup chopped
Soy sauce   3 tablespoons
Lemon juice   2 tablespoons
Rack of lamb   8-bone size, back fat removed

1. Combine wine, nuoc mam, oregano, thyme, and pepper. Stir in onion, garlic, parsley, soy sauce, and lemon juice. Place rack of lamb in glass or ceramic container; pour marinade on top. Refrigerate overnight, turning rack occasionally.
2. Remove meat from marinade. Slice down between bones of rack, but do not cut through completely. Preheat oven to 500 to 525°.
3. Strain marinade. Place herbs, onions, etc. in bottom of roasting pan. Cover with fresh merlot. Place lamb in pan; set into oven and bake for 20 minutes. Baste occasionally. Turn rack and roast for another 15 minutes. Degrease pan juices and serve with lamb. Serve hot.

Serves 4

Leg of Lamb with Walla Walla Onion and Herb Stuffing

Fresh lamb becomes available each year at about the time the first Walla Walla onions reach the market. The delicate taste of northwest lamb and the sweetness of the onions go very well together. Accompany this dish with a good Yakima Valley merlot or lemberger.

Leg of lamb   1, boned
Medium Walla Walla onions   2, sliced
Ripe Yakima tomatoes   2, sliced
Large green bell pepper   1, sliced
Salt and freshly ground black pepper   to taste
Olive oil   3 tablespoons
Garlic cloves   3 to 6, minced (or more, depending on preference)
Bay leaves   2
Parsley sprig   1, finely chopped
Thyme sprig   1, finely chopped
Small sweet turnips*   8
Merlot wine   1 cup

1. Wash meat and remove fell. (The fell is the thin, semiopaque membrane covering the leg of lamb.) Trim excess fat and form meat into large bag by sewing bottom and 2 sides together with butcher twine.
2. Sprinkle onions, tomatoes, and bell pepper with salt and pepper and arrange in alternating layers in the pocket. Fasten opening securely with skewers. Rub surface of meat with salt and pepper.
3. Heat olive oil in a large cast-iron dutch oven or other heavy kettle. Add garlic, bay leaves, parsley, and thyme; cook for 2 minutes, then add lamb and brown on all sides, turning carefully (for about 20 minutes).
4. Add turnips and wine, cover, and bake in 325° oven for 1½ hours. Turn meat occasionally in wine. Serve.

* Use other turnips if you cannot obtain the sweet kind, but the taste will not be quite as exquisite. Sooke, British Columbia, has the best of these.

Serves 8 to 10 (allow ½ pound per person)

Lamb-Stuffed Onion in Fresh Tomato Sauce

The tomatoes for this dish should come from either the Willamette Valley or from the hot valleys east of the mountains to make sure they have ripened properly and are full-flavored. Accompany this dish with a hearty red Yakima Valley wine.

Sweet Walla Walla or Yakima Valley Spanish onions   6
Salted water   as needed
Unsalted butter (see Index)   2 tablespoons
Ground lamb   3½ cups
Light soy sauce   1 teaspoon
Ripe tomatoes   1 cup peeled, seeded, drained, and chopped
Hot paprika   pinch
Red wine vinegar   1 teaspoon
Cheddar cheese   1 cup grated (or more or less, as needed)

1. Peel onions. Place in large pan with 1 inch of salted water. Cover and bring to a boil. Simmer 10 to 15 minutes, or until just tender. Drain.
2. Cut a ½-inch slice from top of onions. Scoop out center, leaving a ½-inch-thick shell. Drain well (place upside down on paper towels).
3. Melt butter in heavy skillet. Chop leftover onion. Measure out ⅓ cup and mix with ground lamb. Add to pan and stir until lamb is lightly cooked. Stir in soy sauce and tomato. Cook for 1 minute. Add paprika and vinegar. Stir well.
4. Spoon mixture into onion shells. Cover with grated cheese. Bake in 350° oven for 20 to 30 minutes or until heated through and cheese has melted.

Serves 6

Lamb-Stuffed Eggplant

This dish is very good with a rich merlot from eastern Washington, or with a Yakima Valley lemberger. Or, if you don't like red wine with your food, try it with a pinot noir blanc. Use extrasharp Bandon or Rogue River white Cheddar, or Cascadian goat cheese from Briar Hills in Chehalis.

Large eggplant   1
Salt   as needed
Hot or mild paprika   as needed
Lemon juice   from ½ lemon
Garlic clove   1, crushed
Ground (or chopped) lamb   1 cup cooked
Bread crumbs   4 tablespoons
Parsley   1 teaspoon finely chopped
Rosemary   1 teaspoon finely chopped
Basil   1 teaspoon finely chopped
Garlic cloves   4, finely chopped
Nuoc mam   ¼ teaspoon
Ripe tomatoes   1 cup peeled, seeded, drained, and chopped
Unsalted butter (see Index)   1 tablespoon
Cheddar cheese   ¼ cup grated

1. Halve eggplant lengthwise. Scoop out pulp (being careful not to cut through the skin), leaving ¾-inch-thick shells. Sprinkle inside of shells with salt, paprika, and lemon juice. Rub outside with crushed garlic clove.
2. Cook pulp in boiling water until tender. Drain and mash. Add next 8 ingredients. Fill eggplant shells with mixture. Dot with butter and sprinkle with cheese. Bake in 375° oven for 30 minutes.

Serves 2 to 4

Spring Kid with Fresh Bracken Shoots

Kid is an exceptionally tasty meat which is finally receiving the popularity it deserves. It was sometimes hard to find in the past, but nowadays a ready supply is available every spring as goat dairies sell off surplus kids. Serve with a rich red wine or a premium porter or stout.

Bracken shoots   16 to 24, cleaned of brown fuzz
Kid scallops cut from loin   8 to 12
Freshly ground black pepper   to taste
Flour   ¼ cup sifted
Unsalted butter (see Index)   3 tablespoons
Olive oil   3 tablespoons
Dry red wine   ⅓ cup
Lamb stock or chicken (see Index) or turkey stock   ⅓ cup
Nuoc mam or light soy sauce   1 teaspoon
Cascadian goat cheese   8 to 12 thin slices

1. Cook bracken shoots in boiling water until tender-crisp (about 5 to 7 minutes). Refresh in cold water. Set aside.
2. Pound kid scallops as thin as possible between sheets of waxed paper. Season with pepper. Pat with flour, shaking off excess.
3. Heat butter and oil in heavy skillet. When hot, brown kid over high heat for 1 minute on each side. Transfer kid to a large baking pan that can accommodate meat in single layer.
4. Pour excess fat from frying pan; deglaze pan with wine; add stock and nuoc mam. Reduce pan juice by half.
5. Top each slice of kid with 2 bracken shoots (the fiddleheads curling in opposite directions), dividing evenly, and 1 slice of cheese. Spoon a little sauce over each scallop.
6. Seal pan with foil. Bake in 425° preheated oven for 10 minutes.

Serves 4 to 6

Loin of Kid with Pasta

Unfortunately, kid is not eaten as much in our region as it should be, mostly due to a popular misconception that "goat" has a strong off-taste. While this may be true for old battle-worn billy goats, it is certainly not true for young females and for kid. Kid grown in the cool climate of the Pacific Northwest undergoes less stress and is thus tastier than kid raised in hot climes. Tender young kid (sometimes sold as "chevon") is widely available from goat dairies each spring. You should plan to make your own slaughtering and cutting arrangements: just look up a custom slaughterer in your Yellow Pages, or have the dairy people help you with finding a reliable butcher. The ancient kings of Navarre accompanied their Easter kid with the rich, golden wine of Jurançon—try it with a fruity northwest muscat instead.

Milk-fed kid loins   two, 2 pounds each, trimmed and boned
Lemon juice   1 cup
Lemon thyme sprigs   2
Olive oil   2 cups
Salt   ½ teaspoon
Coarsely ground black pepper   ½ teaspoon
Garlic cloves   4, crushed
Unsalted butter (see Index)   2 tablespoons
Medium onions   2, diced
Medium carrots   2, diced
Celery stalks   2, diced
Muscat wine   1 cup
Morel mushrooms or cultivated oyster mushrooms   1 cup chopped
Unsalted butter (see Index)   1 tablespoon (or more, as needed)
Salt and freshly ground black pepper   to taste
Chinese oyster sauce   2 teaspoons
Fresh pasta   1 pound
Crisp-cooked spring asparagus   1 to 2 pounds

1. Beat kid loin to flatten slightly. Marinate for 1 hour in covered ceramic or glass dish in mixture of lemon juice, lemon thyme, oil, salt, pepper, and garlic, turning kid every 10 minutes.
2. Remove and drain kid; pat dry with paper towels.
3. In heavy pot, heat 2 tablespoons butter. Brown kid lightly in butter. Remove and keep warm. Sauté onions in butter until golden. Add kid, remaining vegetables, and wine. Cover tightly and place in preheated 350° oven for 1½ to 2 hours, until cooked, but still pink inside. Baste frequently with pan juices.
4. Remove loin from pot to serving platter; keep warm.
5. In the meantime, sauté morels in 1 tablespoon butter; season with salt and pepper.
6. Strain pan juices to remove vegetables. Puree vegetables in food mill or food processor. Skim fat from pan juices. Blend vegetables back into degreased pan juices; blend in morels and oyster sauce. Cook fresh pasta (about 30 seconds) and drain.
7. Add pasta to vegetable mixture, tossing to coat well. Season with extra salt and pepper, if desired.

8. Slice kid loins into ½-inch slices; lay on top of pasta. Cover and reheat. Serve hot with fresh asparagus.

Serves 6 to 8

Surf 'n' Turf

Commonly, when talking about "surf 'n' turf," diners think of that standard American middle-class dish, steak and lobster. I find the following version more interesting. Accompany this with a hearty ale, stout, or porter, or take your chances and drink a robust red jug wine.

Cornstarch   2 teaspoons
Dry sherry   1½ tablespoons
Light soy sauce   2 tablespoons
Milk-fed kid loin   1 pound, thinly sliced against the grain into 2-inch-long pieces
Vegetable oil   3 tablespoons
Thin asparagus   1 pound, sliced diagonally into ½-inch slices
Geoduck belly meat   1 pound, cleaned and thinly sliced crosswise
Nuoc mam   1 teaspoon
Chicken stock (see Index)   3 tablespoons

1. Combine cornstarch, sherry, and soy sauce. Drop kid into marinade and coat evenly; then let stand and marinate for 10 minutes.
2. Heat 1½ tablespoons of oil in a wok or heavy skillet over a high flame and stir-fry kid just long enough to brown meat lightly. Remove from pan and let drain.
3. Add remaining 1½ tablespoons oil to pan. When hot, drop in first asparagus, then geoduck. Stir-fry for a few seconds to coat with oil. Add nuoc mam and stock; let mixture boil until asparagus is crisp-tender, about 1 minute.
4. Add kid and combine with asparagus and geoduck by tossing. Serve hot.

Serves 5 to 6

Dutch Oven Pot Roast

The dutch oven is basically a heavy cast-iron pot with short legs and a heavy lid that has a low rim, allowing hot coals to be piled on top. It traveled west with the first pioneers who settled the Oregon country, and it is still in wide use today, particularly among the lonely hunters, fishermen, sheepherders, and cowboys who travel through the empty lands of the Cascades and the eastern deserts. The dutch oven is a great tool for fireplace cookery—a definite boon when a sudden winter storm has knocked out your supply of electrical power and you expect guests for dinner. Here's a simple fireplace recipe that will make everyone happy, no matter how hard it blows outside.

Beef roast (eye of round, shoulder, chuck, blade, or brisket)   1, of a size to fit your dutch
    oven with space between the roast and the lid (trim roast if necessary)
Warm water or beef stock   ½ cup
Large carrots   4, chunked
Potatoes   4, peeled and chunked
Small onions   4, quartered
Garlic cloves   6 to 12, as desired
Whole allspice   4
Salt and coarsely ground black pepper   to taste

1. Braise roast in water in dutch oven while a lusty hardwood fire burns on the hearth.
2. Add remaining ingredients. Tightly close lid (you might want to glue down the lid with dough to conserve heat and moisture inside dutch oven).
3. When fire has burned down into coals, set dutch oven into a bed of hot coals. Cover lid with hot coals. Pile as many coals as possible against side of pot. Make sure coals continue to burn slowly. Leave to cook all day. Meat should be ready and very tender by dinnertime.

Note: To make dough for sealing lid, just mix water and flour until you get a paste the consistency of putty. Then form it into a long strip and place it around the lip of the pot. Put lid on top and press dough into any remaining cracks.

Serves 4 to 6

Oregon Blue Cheese-Stuffed Burgers

Northwesterners, like other people across the country, eat their share of ground beef patties. I don't eat much ground beef myself, and I had forgotten how good a hamburger can be until I had one last spring on the Skagit Valley farm of Lynn and Margaret Weidenbach. But this one was special—the ground round came from a grain-fed Charolais heifer. Here's a recipe good for doctoring up some less sublimely perfect ground beef.

Ground beef   1½ pounds
Salt   to taste
Freshly ground black pepper   ¼ teaspoon
Cream cheese (see Index)   1½ ounces
Oregon blue cheese   1 tablespoon crumbled
Medium onion   1, minced
Prepared horseradish   1 teaspoon

1. Sprinkle ground beef with salt and pepper; mix lightly but thoroughly.
2. Divide meat into 8 equal portions and form into patties 4 inches in diameter.
3. Combine cream cheese (it helps to press the fresh cheese lightly for about an hour or so to extract extra moisture), blue cheese, onion, and horseradish.
4. Place 1 tablespoon of mixture in center of each of 4 patties. Top with remaining patties. Press edges together securely to seal.
5. Place on grill over ash-covered coals so burgers are 5 to 6 inches from coals. Broil 5 to 6 minutes on first side, turn, and broil 5 to 6 minutes, to doneness desired.

Serves 4

St. Paddy's Day Corned Beef and Vegetable Stew

Here's a solid stew to fortify you against the last of the winter weather, the spring blues, and all that heavy celebrating taking place amongst our region's ethnic and honorary Gaels. This stew is best accompanied by a hearty northwest ale or stout (Guiness will do in a pinch) or by some good handmade whiskey. The original recipe calls for carrots as one of the ingredients, but we have left them out: our Irish friends feel that no orange should be seen on Saint Paddy's day!

Corned beef brisket   2½ to 3½ pounds
Water or beer and water   as needed
Potatoes   2 cups diced
Broccoli florets and slices   1 pound
Medium turnip   1, thinly julienned
Lemon thyme leaves   1 teaspoon chopped
Parsley   2 teaspoons chopped
Freshly ground black pepper   ¼ teaspoon
Dill   ½ teaspoon chopped

1. Place brisket in dutch oven; add water (or ½ beer, ¾ water) to cover. Cover tightly and simmer 2½ to 3½ hours, or until meat is tender.
2. Remove 1 cup cooking liquid 30 minutes before brisket is done and place in saucepan over high heat. Add potatoes and cook over medium heat for 15 minutes. Add broccoli, turnip, and herbs; cover tightly and cook another 12 to 15 minutes, or until potatoes are tender.
3. Carve brisket diagonally across the grain into thin slices and serve with vegetables and broth.

Makes 3 servings per pound of meat

Sausage-Stuffed Apples

This dish calls for a high-quality custom-made sausage like that made by Warren Dimmick in Burlington or Fred Bucheli in Yakima. Make sure to use baking apples, otherwise your "shells" may turn out too soft and mushy. Accompany this dish with a premium lager beer.

Tart baking apples   6
Seasoned pork sausage   2 to 3 pounds (exact quantity depends on size of apples)
Sauerkraut (preferably homemade)   ½ pound

1. Slice off top of apples and core apples, leaving only a thick casing.
2. Dice apple pulp and mix well with sausage.
3. Stuff apple cases with a layer of sausage (⅓), a layer of sauerkraut, and another layer of sausage. Pile final layer of sausage high.
4. Bake in a 375° oven for 35 to 40 minutes. Serve hot.

Serves 4 to 6

Rauner Family Barbecue Sauce

This recipe comes from Louise Rauner, wife of Yakima River Winery wine maker John Rauner. Try it with spareribs, lamb, kid, or beef.

Soy sauce   16-ounce bottle
Basil   2 tablespoons
Rosemary   2 tablespoons
Sugar   ¼ cup
Dry mustard   2 tablespoons
Small Walla Walla sweet onion   1, minced
Olive oil   2 tablespoons
Yakima River merlot   6 ounces
Freshly ground black pepper   1 tablespoon

Place ingredients in saucepan and simmer a few minutes. Cool. It is now ready to use.

Note: For spareribs, use sauce as a topping. Place ribs in a pan, cover with sauce, and cover pan with foil while cooking. Or use sauce as a barbecue basting sauce (it works very well with kid and lamb).

Makes 2¾ cups

Baked Goods
and
Desserts

Basque Sheepherder's Bread

The sheepherder's wagon of eastern Oregon, a tidy, horse-drawn contraption containing the sheepherder's bed, clothes bin, stove, and pantry, must be one of the most efficient traveling carts designed before the age of the motorized camper (the Klamath Falls museum has an excellent specimen). While there was sufficient space for the sheepherder and his togs in the wagon, there really was no room for cooking. Much of the cooking was done over the open fire and the daily bread, called "big bread" by the Basque shepherds, was baked in a dutch oven buried in the ground (for extra insulation). The process was, and still is, very simple (and may be done in your very own backyard): dig a two-foot hole in the ground and light a wood fire (the shepherds perform this task long before daylight). While the fire is burning down to coals, ready the bread dough. Needless to say, Sheepherder's Bread goes very well with fresh lamb chops (flavored with wild sage and other desert herbs, of course) and a lusty red wine.

Milk   1 cup
Cold water   2 cups
Vegetable oil or butter   3 tablespoons
Yeast   2 packages
Warm water   ¼ cup
Sugar   1½ tablespoons
Salt   2½ teaspoons
Flour   9½ cups unsifted
Sourdough starter*   2 tablespoons

1. The night before, combine milk, cold water, and oil; bring to a boil, then cool to lukewarm. Dissolve yeast in warm water; add with sugar and salt to cooled mixture.
2. Pour flour into large bowl, make a crater in center, and pour mixture into hole. Add starter and stir until blended, but do not knead.
3. Put dough into greased bowl, cover, and let rise until morning.
4. When fire has burned down to coals, place dough in well-greased 10-inch dutch oven. Seal lid with dough (see Index) or aluminum foil to prevent dirt from spoiling bread. Shovel excess embers from hole, leaving an inch-thick bed on the bottom. Set dutch oven onto bed of coals, shovel hot embers around and on top of pot, cover with dirt.
5. Do as the shepherds do and forget the entire thing until nightfall. Carefully dig out the dutch oven and, voilà, fresh bread.

* You can substitute 2 packets of active dry yeast if you don't have any sourdough starter on hand.

Makes 1 large loaf

Beer Bread

In our part of the Northwest, this seems to be one of the more popular party breads, especially for summer lamb and kid roasts and beer parties. It is very easy to make.

Flour   3 cups
Baking powder   4½ teaspoons
Salt   1½ teaspoons
Sugar   1½ tablespoons
Lager beer   12-ounce can

1. Combine ingredients and mix well.
2. Pour batter into greased loaf pan. Place in a cold oven set at 375°. Bake for approximately 1 hour.
3. Remove from oven and brush top with butter; return to oven for 10 additional minutes.
4. Cool, wrap, and refrigerate for 24 hours (this helps get rid of the baking powder taste, among other things).
5. Slice, toast, and serve.

Makes 1 loaf

Fried Bread

This recipe was given to me by Sharon Wolf of the Lummi tribe, who likes to eat it with a variety of foods, from clams and salmon to homemade jams.

Warm water   1¾ cups
Flour   4¼ cups
Salt   1 teaspoon
Baking powder   1 tablespoon
Powdered milk   2 tablespoons

1. Combine water with dry ingredients and mix well. Knead mixture for about 5 minutes.
2. Allow dough to rise in a covered bowl for 30 to 45 minutes.
3. Pat dough into 6- to 8-inch circles and fry in golden oil until lightly browned and slightly puffed.

Makes 4 to 6

Wild Blackberry Pie

This recipe comes from Rick O'Reilly of La Petite Maison in Olympia. Our native dewberry gets its special taste from the unique combination of northwest soils and climate, making it a treat that few people outside the Northwest have ever enjoyed.

Cornstarch   2½ tablespoons
Sugar   1 cup (if berries are very ripe, use only ⅔ cup)
Cinnamon   ½ teaspoon
Blackberries   3 to 4 cups, brushed clean (do not wash)
Pâte Brisée
Unsalted butter (see Index)   2 tablespoons

1. Toss cornstarch with sugar and cinnamon; then toss sugar mixture with berries.
2. Place mixture in crust. Dot with pieces of butter and cover with second crust. Seal edges of crust well. Cut decorative slits in top crust. Place pie on rimmed cookie sheet to catch any drips and bake in 400° oven 40 to 50 minutes.

Serves 8

Pâte Brisée

Flour   2⅔ cups
Unsalted butter (see Index)   1 cup, well chilled, cut into ½-inch pieces
Salt   1 teaspoon
Very cold water   ½ cup

1. Blend flour, butter, and salt until a coarse meal is formed. (You should be able to see pieces of butter in the mixture; this will assure a flaky crust.)
2. Add water and mix just until flour is bound and all water is absorbed. Don't add more water if mixture seems dry. Instead, bind mixture by dumping half of it onto a piece of plastic wrap or into a plastic bag. Pull corners of plastic wrap together and press dough firmly, flattening it into a 5-inch disk. Place in refrigerator to chill. Repeat with remaining dough.
3. After thorough chilling, roll dough out on a lightly floured surface to desired size. Place first dough round in pie pan and prick with fork to prevent bubbling. Remember to moisten edge of crust in pan so that after crust is filled and top crust is set in place crimping of edges will seal. Remember also to prick top crust after edges are sealed.

Note: Rick O'Reilly offers these basic rules for making a perfect crust:
   1. Use cold butter;
   2. Use just enough water to bind flour; too much water will toughen the crust;
   3. Allow dough to rest in refrigerator for ½ hour;
   4. Roll out dough quickly on a cool surface; and
   5. Don't overhandle the dough; again, it will toughen if you do.

Makes 2 single crusts

Blueberry and Cream Pie

This recipe comes from Joy Hughes of the Eastview Blueberry Farm in Ferndale, Washington. It is best when made with luscious Whatcom County blueberries.

Blueberries   4 cups
Unbaked 9-inch pastry shell   1
Sugar   ⅔ cup
Flour   ¼ cup
Cinnamon   ½ teaspoon
Salt   ¼ teaspoon
Heavy cream   ½ cup
Milk   ½ cup
Sweetened whipped cream   1 cup
Blueberries and mint leaves   garnish

1. Preheat oven to 400°. Pour blueberries into pastry shell.
2. In small bowl, combine sugar, flour, cinnamon, and salt. Stir in heavy cream and milk with wire whisk until smooth. Pour mixture over berries.
3. Bake for 45 minutes. If edge gets too brown, cover with strips of foil. Cool on wire rack. Refrigerate. Serve garnished with sweetened whipped cream. Decorate with blueberries and mint leaves.

Serves 8

Wild Blueberry Pie

You've got to go high in the mountains to pick the small low-bush blueberries for this pie, but the final result is well worth the effort.

Baked 9-inch pie shell   1
Wild blueberries   4 cups
Sugar   1 cup
Cornstarch   3 tablespoons
Salt   ¼ teaspoon
Water   ¼ cup
Unsalted butter (see Index)   1 tablespoon

1. Line cooled pie shell with 2 cups blueberries.
2. Cook remaining berries with sugar, cornstarch, salt, and water over medium heat until thickened. Remove from heat, add butter and pour over berries in shell. Chill until ready to serve.

Serves 8

Blueberry Syrup

Serve this syrup warm or chilled over waffles, pancakes, ice cream, crêpes, et al.

Ripe blueberries   2 cups
Sugar   ⅓ to ½ cup (depending on personal taste and sweetness of blueberries)

Place blueberries and sugar in container of blender or food processor. Process until smooth. Pour into saucepan; bring to boil and cook, stirring constantly for 5 minutes. You may strain syrup through a fine sieve if you want a very smooth, seedless syrup.

Makes 2 cups

Blueberry Coffee Cake

Here is another recipe from Joy Hughes of the Eastview Blueberry Farm.

Sugar   ¾ cup
Shortening   ¼ cup
Egg   1, lightly beaten
Milk   ½ cup
Flour   2 cups
Baking powder   2 teaspoons
Salt   ¼ teaspoon
Blueberries   2 cups
Brown sugar   ½ cup
Flour   ⅓ cup
Unsalted butter (see Index)   ¼ cup

1. Cream sugar and shortening; add egg, and stir in milk. Sift flour, baking powder, and salt; add to creamed mixture. Stir in blueberries. Place mixture in greased 8-inch-square baking pan.
2. Combine brown sugar, flour, and butter and sprinkle crumbly mixture over cake mixture.
3. Bake at 375° for 35 to 45 minutes. Cool before serving.

Serves 6 to 12

Blueberry Crêpes

This is one of the more elegant recipes in Joy Hughes's Eastview Farm recipe collection.

Blueberries 1½ cups
Sugar ½ cup
Cornstarch 1 tablespoon
Nutmeg ¼ teaspoon
Lemon juice 1 tablespoon
Basic Dessert Crêpes 6 to 8, cooked
Vanilla ice cream

1. In saucepan, combine blueberries, sugar, cornstarch, nutmeg, and lemon juice. Cook, stirring constantly, until thickened. Cool 5 to 10 minutes.
2. Fill each crêpe with scoops of ice cream. Fold over. Spoon warm sauce over filled crêpes. Serve immediately.

Serves 4 to 6

Basic Dessert Crêpes

Eggs 4
Flour 1 cup
Sugar 2 tablespoons
Milk 1 cup
Water ¼ cup
Unsalted butter (see Index) 1 tablespoon, melted

1. In medium mixing bowl, beat eggs. Gradually add flour and sugar alternately with milk and water, beating with wire whisk or electric mixer until smooth. Beat in melted butter.
2. Refrigerate batter for at least 1 hour.
3. Cook in lightly greased pan, pouring batter into pan for each crêpe, and pouring excess batter back into bowl each time.

Makes about 20 to 25 crêpes

Joy Hughes's Honey-Blueberry Muffins

This dish makes a good dessert for a country dinner, but it can also make a satisfying light breakfast.

Flour   2 cups
Salt   ½ teaspoon
Baking powder   1 tablespoon
Milk   1 cup
Blueberry honey   ¼ cup
Egg   1, beaten
Blueberries   ½ cup
Shortening   ¼ cup, melted

1. Sift flour with salt and baking powder. Mix milk, honey, egg, blueberries, and shortening. Add to dry ingredients. Fill greased muffin pans half full with mixture.
2. Bake at 400° for 35 minutes or until golden brown.

Makes 12 muffins

Joy Hughes's Blubarb Jam

This is an excellent jam. It combines two of our best products, blueberries and rhubarb.

Rhubarb   3 cups finely cut
Sugar   7 cups
Blueberries   3 cups crushed
Liquid fruit pectin   6-ounce bottle

1. Simmer rhubarb gently until tender. Combine with sugar in large saucepan; add blueberries. Mix.
2. Place over high heat. Bring to full boil and boil hard 1 minute, stirring constantly. Remove from heat; add pectin. Stir and skim for 5 minutes.
3. Ladle into hot sterilized glasses. Cover at once.

Makes about 9 half pints

Apple Bread

This is a simple, but very tasty sweet bread. Accompany it with a late-harvest riesling or gewürztraminer.

Cooking apples   4 cups cored, peeled, and diced
Unsalted butter (see Index)   1 cup, melted
Sugar   2 cups
Pastry flour   2 cups
Large eggs   2
Salt   to taste
Cinnamon   2 teaspoons
Hazelnuts   ½ cup chopped and toasted

1. Mix all ingredients together in large work bowl.
2. Pour batter into greased 9- by 5-inch bread pan; bake at 350° for about 1 hour.

Makes 1 loaf

Pear Soufflé with Loganberry Sauce

Sinclair Philip at the Sooke Harbour House likes to use local fruits in his desserts. For this recipe he used locally grown pears—tarter than the ones from east of the Cascades—and Sooke loganberries. Accompany this dish with a rich late-harvest wine or with a sweet liqueur.

Ripe pears   2, peeled, cored, and halved
Very dry pear or plum brandy   2 tablespoons
Egg whites   2
Dessert Crêpes
Loganberry Sauce

1. Poach pears in small amount of water until very soft. Drain and let cool. Then puree pears in blender or food processor fitted with steel blade, adding brandy.
2. Preheat oven to 425°.
3. Whip egg whites until very stiff and gently fold into pear puree.
4. Place crêpes in center of individual oven-proof plates and spoon pear mixture onto the first half, then fold other half over mixture.
5. Evenly distribute sauce around each crêpe. Set plates on top shelf of hot oven for 5 minutes until soufflé has browned a little. Serve on doilied plates. (Plates will be extremely hot.)

Note: To flambé, prewarm 2 ounces of very dry pear or plum brandy. When hot, pour over crêpes and immediately set on fire. Do not allow brandy to run into pureed fruit mixture surrounding the crêpe.

Serves 4

Dessert Crêpes

Egg yolks   2
Sugar   1 tablespoon
Cold water   ¼ cup
Cold milk   ¼ cup
Flour   ¼ cup
Unsalted butter (see Index)   2 tablespoons, melted
Orange liqueur   1 tablespoon

1. Place ingredients in work bowl of blender or food processor. Process until well combined.
2. Cover and refrigerate for a few hours.
3. Cook in lightly greased pan, pouring batter into pan for each crêpe, and pouring excess batter back into bowl each time.

Makes four 5-inch crêpes

Loganberry Sauce

Ripe loganberries   2 cups
Lemon juice   1 tablespoon

Puree berries and juice in blender and set aside.

Makes about 2 cups

Pears and Raspberries over Ice Cream

This is a midsummer dish, a dessert at its best when it is possible to use both newly ripened summer Bartletts and fresh raspberries. But one may also enjoy it in winter with luscious Oregon Comice pears and home-frozen raspberries. Use a very rich, sweet late-harvest riesling or gewürztraminer in the cooking, and accompany the dish with more of the same wine.

Dessert riesling or gewürztraminer   1 cup
Sugar   ⅛ to ¼ cup (depending on sweetness of wine)
Pure vanilla extract   1 teaspoon
Medium-sized ripe summer Bartlett pears   4
Raspberries   2 cups
Poire William brandy or plum brandy   2 tablespoons
Premium (preferably homemade) vanilla ice cream   4 scoops
Mint leaves   garnish

1. In 10-inch skillet, combine wine, sugar, and vanilla. Bring to boil; add pears. Cover and simmer until tender, about 8 to 10 minutes, turning pears once (reduce cooking time in winter when using very ripe Comice pears).
2. Press 1½ cups raspberries through fine sieve. Add raspberry juice to liquid in pan. Boil hard to reduce to ⅓ cup (8 to 10 minutes). Remove from heat. Add pear brandy (you may flame brandy if you go in for fireworks).
3. To serve, place a generous scoop of ice cream in each of 4 sherbet dishes. Make a slight depression in top of each scoop with back of spoon. Place 3 to 4 mint leaves on rim of each crater. Set 1 pear upright in each crater atop each scoop of ice cream; spoon remaining ½ cup fresh raspberries around base of pear. Divide syrup and dribble over pear and raspberries. Serve immediately.

Serves 4

Cranberry Fool

The Shelburne Inn is located in Seaview, more or less in the heart of the Washington cranberry growing region. This dessert shows what Ann Kischner, the restaurant's pastry and dessert chef, can do with the local product.

Cranberries   1 pound
Sugar   1 cup
Orange juice   1 cup
Whipping cream   2 cups

Boil together cranberries, sugar, and orange juice until berries split open. Puree and strain. Allow to cool until it begins to set up. Whip cream until fairly stiff. Fold cranberry mixture into cream. Divide and put into stemmed glasses. Garnish with whole cranberries. Chill well before serving.

Serves 6 to 8

U.S. and Metric Measurements

Approximate conversion formulas are given below for commonly used U.S. and metric kitchen measurements.

Teaspoons	x	5	= milliliters
Tablespoons	x	15	= milliliters
Fluid ounces	x	30	= milliliters
Fluid ounces	x	0.03	= liters
Cups	x	240	= milliliters
Cups	x	0.24	= liters
Pints	x	0.47	= liters
Dry pints	x	0.55	= liters
Quarts	x	0.95	= liters
Dry quarts	x	1.1	= liters
Gallons	x	3.8	= liters
Ounces	x	28	= grams
Ounces	x	0.028	= kilograms
Pounds	x	454	= grams
Pounds	x	0.45	= kilograms
Milliliters	x	0.2	= teaspoons
Milliliters	x	0.07	= tablespoons
Milliliters	x	0.034	= fluid ounces
Milliliters	x	0.004	= cups
Liters	x	34	= fluid ounces
Liters	x	4.2	= cups
Liters	x	2.1	= pints
Liters	x	1.82	= dry pints
Liters	x	1.06	= quarts
Liters	x	0.91	= dry quarts
Liters	x	0.26	= gallons
Grams	x	0.035	= ounces
Grams	x	0.002	= pounds
Kilograms	x	35	= ounces
Kilograms	x	2.2	= pounds

Temperature Equivalents

Fahrenheit	− 32	× 5	÷ 9	= Celsius
Celsius	× 9	÷ 5	+ 32	= Fahrenheit

U.S. Equivalents

1 teaspoon	= ⅓ tablespoon
1 tablespoon	= 3 teaspoons
2 tablespoons	= 1 fluid ounce
4 tablespoons	= ¼ cup or 2 ounces
5⅓ tablespoons	= ⅓ cup or 2⅔ ounces
8 tablespoons	= ½ cup or 4 ounces
16 tablespoons	= 1 cup or 8 ounces
⅜ cup	= ¼ cup plus 2 tablespoons
⅝ cup	= ½ cup plus 2 tablespoons
⅞ cup	= ¾ cup plus 2 tablespoons
1 cup	= ½ pint or 8 fluid ounces
2 cups	= 1 pint or 16 fluid ounces
1 liquid quart	= 2 pints or 4 cups
1 liquid gallon	= 4 quarts

Metric Equivalents

1 milliliter	= 0.001 liter
1 liter	= 1000 milliliters
1 milligram	= 0.001 gram
1 gram	= 1000 milligrams
1 kilogram	= 1000 grams

Index

Notes

Other Cookbooks from Pacific Search Press

American Wood Heat Cookery (2d Ed. Revised & Enlarged) by Margaret Byrd Adams
The Apple Cookbook by Kyle D. Fulwiler
The Bean Cookbook: Dry Legume Cookery by Norma S. Upson
The Berry Cookbook by Kyle D. Fulwiler
Canning and Preserving without Sugar by Norma M. MacRae, R.D.
The Crawfish Cookbook by Norma S. Upson
Eating Well: A Guide to Foods of the Pacific Northwest by John Doerper
The Eggplant Cookbook by Norma S. Upson
A Fish Feast by Charlotte Wright
Food 101: A Student Guide to Quick and Easy Cooking by Cathy Smith
One Potato, Two Potato: A Cookbook by Constance Bollen and Marlene Blessing
River Runners' Recipes by Patricia Chambers
The Salmon Cookbook by Jerry Dennon
Starchild & Holahan's Seafood Cookbook by Adam Starchild and James Holahan
The Whole Grain Bake Book by Gail L. Worstman
Wild Mushroom Recipes by the Puget Sound Mycological Society
The Zucchini Cookbook (3d Ed. Revised & Enlarged) by Paula Simmons